Writing a Research Paper
A Step-By-Step Approach

Third Edition

Phyllis Goldenberg

PROGRAM CONSULTANTS

Rose DePoto
Chair of Language Arts
New Milford High School
New Milford, NJ

Linda Anderson
English Language Arts Instructional Coach
Morgan Road Middle School
Hephzibah, GA

Paul R. Sanfrancesco
Director of Technology
Garnet Valley School District
Glen Mills, PA

Sadlier

Acknowledgments

The publisher wishes to thank the following individuals for their suggestions for and contributions to the third edition of *Writing a Research Paper*.

Curriculum Reviewers

Sharon Lathrop
Our Lady of Grace School
El Cajon, California

Douglas Packer
Jane Addams High School
Bronx, New York

Frederick J. Panzer, Sr.
Christopher Columbus High School
Miami, Florida

Thomas J. Pasko
Saint Ignatius High School
Cleveland, Ohio

Patricia Stack
South Park School District
South Park, Pennsylvania

Image Credits

King Features Syndicate: 77, 138, 149. Library of Congress, Rare Book & Special Collections Reading Room/The Alfred Whital Stern Collection of Lincolniana: 106. NPR.org/James A. Chambers, U.S. Army Deputy, Office of the Chief, Military Intelligence: 150. United Features Syndicate, Inc.: 7, 47, 109. United Press Syndicate: 22, 65, 88, 122.

 is a registered trademark of William H. Sadlier, Inc.

Printed in the United States of America
ISBN: 978-0-8215-8180-3
3 4 5 6 7 8 9 BRR 14 13 12 11

Ten Steps to a Successful Research Paper

Third Edition

The third edition of *Writing a Research Paper: A Step-by-Step Approach* maintains the unique, step-by-step approach of the original: It guides students to complete their papers as they complete the book. It also offers additional instruction and exercises on **electronic citations, Internet research,** and **plagiarism,** acknowledging the major role that computers and the Internet now play in both the research for and writing of student papers. More on all three topics, plus in-depth, interactive tutorials and two additional sample research papers, can be found online at **www.sadlierresearchpaper.com**.

At each step, students are introduced to a key element of the research process. They are then given exercises to help them practice and master that element. Finally, they are asked to apply the element in their own research papers.

In content and method, *Writing a Research Paper* is designed to be equally useful to those students who are writing a research paper for the first time and those who have many such papers behind them. For first-time writers, this book provides a clearly organized plan—from choosing the topic to submitting and publishing the finished paper—as well as a wealth of practical advice. For more-experienced writers, the book will prove a handy review and reference manual, complete with reminders, cautions, and hints for writing successful research papers.

Special Features

NEW!

Special online components: Two model research papers, developed step-by-step, plus additional instruction and exercises on Internet research and plagiarism, are online at www.sadlierresearchpaper.com.

e-writing   Online Research

Practical suggestions help writers hone their computer skills and conduct Internet research more effectively.

Hint! Tips give valuable advice at key points in the process.

Cartoons Chapter openers focus on the lighter side of the writing process.

TIMETABLES

Suggested schedules keep students on track for completing the project.

APPENDICES Three supplements provide information on reference materials, topic ideas across the curriculum, and alternate formats and styles.

☑ Checklist Review

End-of-chapter recaps show what needs to be done at each step.

Contents

🖥 Special Online Features
www.sadlierresearchpaper.com

Interactive Tutorials
• Avoiding Plagiarism
• Evaluating Internet Sources

Ten-Step Model Research Papers
• Informational research paper: Langston Hughes
• I-Search paper: Chicago's Pullman Neighborhood

Foreword

By the time you finish this book, you will have transformed blank sheets of paper into a coherent, fact-filled, smooth-sounding research paper that you can be proud of. In the process, you will become a local expert on the topic you have chosen to write about. You will probably end up knowing a great deal more about your topic than any of your classmates, friends, or family. What you find out about your topic will stay with you a long, long time.

That's the *content*—the information you discover.

Research also involves a *process*—how you go about finding information.

Think of this book as a tool kit and map combined into one handy package. It will give you all the tools—the essential skills—you will need in order to plan and complete your research paper, and it will guide you—that's the map part—every step of the way. Literally, you will complete ten steps in the research process.

As you research and write, you will be working some of the time with a partner or with a small group. You and your classmates will advise and support each other as you compare notes on your progress and discoveries, and you will comment on one another's work. For additional support, go to **www.sadlierresearchpaper.com**. There, you will find two model research papers, developed step-by-step, just like yours, as well as two interactive tutorials offering more guidance on plagiarism and evaluating Internet sources.

If this book belongs to you, keep it. No matter how many research papers you are asked to write in the future, the steps of researching and writing will be the same. The content of your future papers will change, but the process will not.

Are you feeling curious? Nervous? Impatient to begin? You're only ten steps away from your finished research paper, so step right up for Step 1—turn on the computer and have a great time!

Phyllis Goldenberg

For more on choosing a topic, see Step 1 in the two model research papers at **www.sadlierresearchpaper.com**.

STEP 1

Choose a Topic

PEANUTS reprinted with permission of United Features Syndicate, Inc.

So you have to write a research paper. You have just been handed one of the most interesting—and challenging—writing assignments of your school career. To complete the assignment on time, you will need to begin promptly and keep plugging away until you have finished. So let's get started! The first thing you will need to do is decide what you are going to write about.

Before You Begin

☑ Make sure you understand your assignment.

A research paper is a long, formal essay or report that presents information from a number of sources. You will need to know exactly when your paper is due, how long it is supposed to be, and what type of research paper you are expected to write.

LENGTH. Your teacher may specify a paper ranging in length from 1,000 to 2,000 words (sometimes more). You can estimate 250 keyboarded words to a double-spaced page to determine the number of pages of text you will need; later, you can use your word processor's word-count tool to get a sense of your progress. Or your teacher may assign a specific number of pages—five to seven double-spaced pages of text, for example. Listen carefully to the assignment, and exactly follow the specifications (for length, topic, type of paper, and style of documentation).

Keep in mind that whenever you write a report, explain an idea, or write a memo or proposal, your writing is **expository** in nature; that is, your purpose is to inform or explain. You are not telling a story (**narrative** writing) or describing something (**descriptive** writing) or trying to convince someone to do something (**persuasive** writing). In expository writing, your purpose is chiefly to convey information to your reader.

AUDIENCE. Usually, your teacher and your classmates are your audience, but sometimes a research paper can be shared with others who are interested in your topic.

For instance, if you have written a paper about a strong-mayor versus a city-commission form of government, you might read and discuss your paper with a social studies class or send it to your local governing body. If you have written about recent legislation protecting an endangered species, you might share your findings with the school's science club or a local environmental organization.

TYPES OF RESEARCH PAPERS. Research papers, which are sometimes called *term papers,* can be classified according to their major purpose. These three types of research paper differ in important ways.

1. INFORMATIONAL, OR FACTUAL, RESEARCH PAPER. You've been writing this type of research paper ever since you wrote your first report in elementary school. In a traditional informational research paper, you present information from a number of different sources (both print and nonprint) without expressing any of your thoughts or feelings about the topic. There's no place for the first-person pronoun *I* in the informational paper. In fact, if your teacher has assigned an informational research paper, you will probably lose points for expressing your opinion or taking a position on your topic.

An informational research paper is **objective**, which means that it is completely factual and does not express your point of view. Consider, for example, these topics:

OBJECTIVE TOPIC Three states' different age requirements for teenagers to get a driver's license (**facts only**)

OBJECTIVE TOPIC History of U.S. women's professional basketball (**facts only**)

In an informational paper, your assignment is to focus the topic, find the information, and produce an organized and coherent paper. Your aim when writing this kind of paper is to *stick to the facts*.

2. EVALUATIVE, OR ANALYTICAL, RESEARCH PAPER. An evaluative research paper also presents information from a number of different sources, but it goes one step farther. In an evaluative paper, you state your opinion or come to a conclusion about your topic based on the information you have presented in your paper. This statement of opinion or conclusion is called a **claim**. Consider these claims:

CLAIM I think our state should not give driver's licenses to 16-year-olds. (**opinion**)

CLAIM The National Basketball Association should support a women's professional basketball league. (**opinion**)

CLAIM Of all the proposed solutions for increasing voter turnout in this country, only one solution is workable and likely to succeed. (**opinion**)

The topic for an evaluative paper may be a contemporary issue or a problem that interests you. You may compare and contrast two artists or writers, for example, and make a claim about whose work will have lasting value. Make sure that your teacher approves your topic before you start your research process. Your aim when writing this kind of paper is to *make a claim and support it*.

3. I-SEARCH PAPER. An I-Search paper tells the story of how you went about your research and what you discovered. You begin by thinking of a topic that you really want to learn about, often one that affects you personally.

RESEARCH QUESTION How can I become an X-ray technician, and is that a career at which I'm likely to be successful?

An I-Search paper demonstrates a definite organization, with sub-headings, like those that follow, which indicate the structure.

- What I already know
- What I want to find out
- How I went about finding out what I want to know
- What I learned

If you're writing an I-Search paper, your most important sources will be **interviews** with two or three people who are knowledgeable about the subject of your research question. For example, someone researching a career as an X-ray technician might interview a person who works as an X-ray technician and a professor who teaches a course to students learning to become X-ray technicians. A major part of your paper tells what you learned from each interview, and at the end of the I-Search paper, you draw a conclusion based on the information you gathered. Your aim when writing this kind of paper is to *tell your story*.

Managing Your Time

☑ Draw up a project schedule.

A research paper is a long-term assignment. In order to see it through to a successful conclusion, you will need to plan well and keep to a schedule. Indeed, one of the most important aspects of a research paper project is time management—that is, making the most efficient use of the time available to you.

Your teacher will specify a deadline (the date on which your paper is due). You then have from the day the paper is assigned until the due date to research and write it. Therefore, your first order of business should be to draw up a project schedule. The sample timetables on page 10 give you some guidelines on how to pace yourself.

AVOID A TIME TRAP. Many teachers require that you turn in specific materials along the way—for example, an outline and a list of sources. Such minideadlines can actually help you stay focused on your task. Other teachers may assign the research paper, give you some specifications and a due date, and then leave you on your own. In that case, it's completely up to you to manage your time. Don't procrastinate. The due date may seem a long way away, but you've got lots of work to do.

KEEP PLUGGING AWAY. Don't get bogged down in one stage of the writing process, such as writing a thesis statement. If you keep working on your assignment and moving forward through each step, you will be able to meet your deadline.

Research Paper Timetables

The chart below gives four timetables, each keyed to a different due date. Do you have eight weeks to complete your paper? See the second column. Use or adapt the schedule to suit your own research paper.

STEPS 📅 Monday 1	10 weeks	8 weeks	6 weeks	4 weeks
PREWRITING				
1 Choose a topic.	1 week	3 days	2 days	1 day
2 Locate sources.	3 days	3 days	2 days	1 day
3 Take notes.	2 weeks	$1\frac{1}{2}$ weeks	1 week	1 week
4 Write a thesis statement and a title.	3 days	2 days	1 day	1 day
5 Write a final outline.	1 week	1 week	2 days	2 days
DRAFTING				
6 Write the first draft.	$1\frac{1}{2}$ weeks	1 week	1 week	4 days
7 Document sources.	2 days	2 days	1 day	1 day
REVISING				
8 Revise the draft.	2 weeks	$1\frac{1}{2}$ weeks	$1\frac{1}{2}$ weeks	3 days
PROOFREADING/EDITING				
9 Find and correct errors.	2 days	2 days	2 days	1 day
PUBLISHING				
10 Publish your research.	3 days	3 days	3 days	2 days

Choosing a Topic

IF A SPECIFIC TOPIC IS ASSIGNED. Be grateful and get going. Rarely, however, does a teacher require everyone to write on the same topic. When more than one person is working on a specific topic, source materials become hard to find because several people are competing for them. Also, most teachers prefer reading about a variety of topics instead of the same one over and over.

IF THE GENERAL SUBJECT IS ASSIGNED BUT NOT THE SPECIFIC TOPIC. If your teacher assigns a general subject and lets you limit it to a workable topic, part of your job is already done. Limiting is easy once you get started. (See pages 13–15 for examples of and suggestions for cluster diagrams.)

IF IT'S TOTALLY UP TO YOU. This is the usual scenario: Your teacher lets you decide what to write about and simply requires that he or she approves your topic once you have chosen it. It is important to settle on a workable topic as soon as possible because you have a lot of work to do once you have made your choice and had it approved. (See Appendix B for suggestions for topics that might interest you.)

Hint!

You don't have to find the "perfect" topic (it probably doesn't exist anyway). You just have to find a *workable* one.

☑ Choose a workable topic that meets all the following requirements.

1. YOU CAN FIND ENOUGH MATERIAL ON THE TOPIC. Usually, a research assignment calls for at least five diverse sources, some print and some nonprint. Sometimes, for instance, you will be expected to conduct an interview to serve as one of your sources. Avoid choosing a topic that is too recent or too technical; you will have trouble locating information. Once you have chosen a topic, do a quick check in your library or media center (see Step 2) to verify that you can find five or more reliable sources on it.

2. THE TOPIC INTERESTS YOU, AND YOU THINK YOU CAN MAKE IT INTEREST YOUR AUDIENCE. An ideal topic tickles your curiosity. You may know something about it already, but you would like to know more. After all, you are going to spend many weeks immersed in the topic. Ask yourself if you would like to become the class "expert" on this topic.

Take an interest inventory. Start by taking stock of the things you are interested in. List as many as possible. For example, you might include your hobbies; your ambitions and goals; careers you are interested in; places you would like to visit; things you are curious about (ideas; how something works and why); the biggest problems in your community, the country, the world; things you would buy if you had all the money you wanted; some famous people you admire and a word or two about why you admire each.

Look for topic ideas. Explore as many sources as you can for possible research paper topics. Browse through newspapers and magazines. Talk to relatives, friends, and experts. Interview someone. Listen to radio talk shows, National Public Radio, and news shows. Watch TV documentaries and the evening news. Browse through the documentary section of a video store. Browse through a library or bookstore. Check out electronic magazines and newspapers on a computer. Flip through an encyclopedia. Use a search engine to browse for topics on the Internet.

WORKING TOGETHER | **Exercise 1** | **Brainstorming**

Alone or with a partner or small group, brainstorm topics that interest you. On a separate sheet of paper or your computer, make a list of ideas and suggestions, including those that you gathered in your interest inventory. Then review the list, and choose the three topics you would most like to write about.

3. THE TOPIC IS OBJECTIVE, NOT SUBJECTIVE. Remember, an objective topic is factual, not personal. Generally, you will be writing an informational or factual research paper. You are not writing about your opinions, your experiences, your friends and relatives, or your feelings and ideas. These are subjective topics. Here are some examples of each type:

- **OBJECTIVE** Evidence for and against side airbags in cars

- **SUBJECTIVE** My uncle's car accident

- **OBJECTIVE** Signing up voters: techniques for registering new voters

- **SUBJECTIVE** What happened when I tried to register to vote

4. THE TOPIC IS LIMITED ENOUGH TO BE COVERED ADEQUATELY IN THE SPACE AVAILABLE TO YOU. You will need to focus your topic until it's just the right size. You can't, for example, write a research paper on the history of China; you would need a whole book— or several—to cover such a broad subject. Limit, or narrow, your topic to one that can be covered thoroughly in the space you have available. (On pages 13–20, you will learn some techniques for limiting a general subject.) But do not choose a topic so narrow that you can cover it completely in a paragraph or two.

- **TOO GENERAL** Ants

- **STILL TOO GENERAL** Fire ants

- **STILL TOO GENERAL** The evolution of fire ants

- **JUST RIGHT** The invasion of fire ants in the United States

- **TOO LIMITED** What to do if you are stung by a fire ant

- **TOO LIMITED** What a fire ant looks like

Hint!

If you can find a dozen books devoted to your topic, the topic is too broad and general and needs to be limited further. For example, if you choose to write about Native American mythology and find six books on that subject listed in your library's catalog, your topic needs to be narrowed further.

Online Research Use a search engine to browse through the listings on a general topic. All search engines explore the Internet for Web pages containing information about a specified topic. It's up to you to determine which of the listings has the information you need. If you enter the word *karate* in Google, for instance, you will get more than 32 million listings, and they will all be more limited in some way than the general word *karate*. Here are some examples of more-limited topics:

history of karate	USA Karate Foundation
karate training and equipment	other international karate foundations
karate rules and etiquette	Karate Hall of Fame
how karate differs from other martial arts	karate competitions

Clustering

A **cluster diagram** is a doodle with a purpose, a graphic device for limiting a general subject to workable topics. Start by writing the big idea—a broad, general subject—in the middle of a piece of paper, and circle it. Then break the big idea into its parts or into smaller ideas or topics you associate with it. Write each smaller idea, circle it, and draw a line connecting it to the center. Keep going, writing still more limited topics branching outward. Here is an example:

Exercise 2 — Making a Cluster Diagram

In the space below, fill in a cluster diagram of one of the topics you came up with in Exercise 1. Remember, there are no right or wrong clusters. Start with the topic in the middle, and branch out from there. Keep going until you run out of ideas and/or room. Add more circles if you need them.

Topic

STRAIGHT-LINE CLUSTER. A straight-line cluster is another kind of diagram that will help you limit a broad topic. It moves from a broad, general subject (at the top) to ever more limited, narrower topics. Try it. You may find it more useful than the bigger cluster.

French Impressionist Painting

↓

Paintings of Claude Monet

↓

Monet's series of paintings of same subject

↓

Monet's Haystack Paintings 1888–1891

Hint!

Your cluster diagram may look entirely different from those of your classmates, even though you all might start with the same broad, general subject. There are no "right" topics in a cluster diagram. A cluster records your own thoughts as you move from a general idea to narrower topics.

Exercise 3 Limiting Your Topic

Fill in the straight-line cluster diagram here. Start with a general topic, and keep limiting it further and further. Your topic should move from the general at the top to the more and more limited as you approach the bottom. On a separate sheet of paper or your computer, make at least two more of these diagrams, starting each one with a different topic. You may add as many circles as you need until you reach a workable topic.

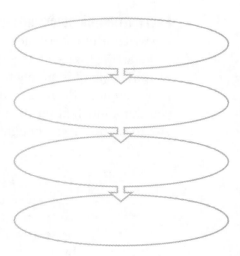

Research Questions

☑ **Word your limited topic as a research question that you are going to investigate.**

Before you start exploring possible sources of information, spend a few minutes jotting down what you already know—or think you know—about your topic. This will help focus your research still further. As you take notes or freewrite, you may end up with one or more research questions—questions to which you would like to find the answers.

TAKING NOTES. Here are some notes made by a student writer for a paper on reforms in the jury system in U.S. courts. The student wrote down everything she already knew and ended by focusing on the research question she wanted to explore.

> Courts use juries in trials to decide whether a person is innocent or guilty as accused. Both criminal and civil. Are there always 12 jurors?
>
> Juries are supposed to be "jury of peers"—a mix of people who represent the population—of ages, races, gender. Are juries mentioned in U.S. Constitution?
>
> How are people called to serve on juries, and what is the source of their names? I think maybe the lists of registered voters or in some places everyone with a driver's license. How old do you have to be?
>
> Who actually gets to choose jurors—the lawyers? the judge?—and how are they chosen?
>
> Cases of innocent people being convicted and guilty people going free.
>
> I'd like to research proposed reforms (changes) in jury system. How can I find out?

FREEWRITING OR QUICKWRITING. Another way to find out what you already know is to freewrite or quickwrite for a few minutes. Keep yourself focused on your topic, and just start writing. Don't worry about complete sentences or connections between ideas. The point is simply to get what's in your brain on paper or onto your computer monitor. Freewriting may contain information as well as questions. Because you think much faster than you write, use abbreviations, fragments, or anything else to capture your thoughts as you focus on your topic.

> Research key words "jury reform" through a search engine and on InfoTrac. See if I can interview Tony's mom, assistant state district attorney. I can write to natl or state Bar Assoc (organization of lawyers) & ask for info about jury reform. Maybe talk with Ben's older brother—graduated from law school last year & was editor of law review. Ask him for advice on how to research the topic—what are best sources?

USING A KWL CHART. Another way to organize your thoughts before you start doing your research is to fill in a KWL chart. In this graphic organizer, you begin by identifying your topic. Then you list what you already *know* about your topic (**K**), what you *want* to know (**W**), and what you *learned* (**L**). You can fill in the first two columns now and complete the third column as you do your research.

Topic: _____

What I Already **K**now	What I **W**ant to Know	What I **L**earned

| Exercise 4 | Identifying Appropriately Limited Topics |

For each numbered item below, identify the topics that are neither too general nor too limited but just right for a 5- to 7-page research paper. On a separate sheet of paper, write the letter(s) of the topic(s) you picked, and explain why you did not pick the others. Some items have more than one correct answer.

1. a. The population of the United States
   b. Information from the latest U.S. census
   c. Some problems in collecting accurate information in the latest U.S. census
   d. The number of people of Vietnamese origin living in San Francisco

2. a. Symbolism in Robert Frost's "Stopping by Woods on a Snowy Evening" and "Mending Wall"
   b. Robert Frost's poetry
   c. Symbolism in contemporary American poetry
   d. The origin of the word *wall*

3. a. Careers in medicine
   b. Pros and cons of being a nurse in a hospital emergency room
   c. The history of medicine in Europe during the twentieth century
   d. Medical research today

4. a. The career of Jackie Robinson, the first African American baseball player in the major leagues
   b. African Americans and baseball
   c. The history of baseball in America
   d. The World Series

5. a. U.S. presidential elections
   b. Pros and cons of paid political advertisements
   c. U.S. presidential candidates
   d. Problems with various types of voting machines

6. a. Harriet Tubman's accomplishments on the Underground Railroad
   b. History of slavery in the Americas
   c. Fugitive slave laws
   d. *Roots* by Alex Haley—tracing the writer's origins back to Africa

7. a. The history of writing
   b. Cracking hieroglyphics—the Rosetta stone
   c. Cuneiform and hieroglyphics—precursors of the alphabet
   d. Sequoya's invention of an alphabet for the Cherokee language

8. a. History of and current requirements for physical education in local schools

   b. Overweight Americans

   c. Too much TV

   d. Health benefits of sports and other forms of exercise

WORKING TOGETHER   **Exercise 5**   **Limiting a Broad Subject**

See how many limited topics appropriate for a research paper you can list for each of the broad, general subjects below. Work with a partner on the first topic. Use a separate sheet of paper or your computer. Here is an example to get you started.

General topic. Dogs

Limited topics. Obedience training; breeds of dogs that are good with children; crime-fighting dogs; how seeing-eye dogs are trained; most dangerous dogs; White House dogs; animal shelters; rabies and other serious diseases; from wolves to dogs—their early history

1. Popular music	**6.** Circuses
2. Space travel	**7.** Television
3. Cartoons	**8.** Careers in science
4. World War II	**9.** Community problems
5. Ancient Greece	**10.** Olympic Games

 Exercise 6   **Freewriting About a Limited Topic**

Choose one of the limited topics you are considering for your paper. On a separate sheet of paper or your computer, freewrite for several minutes about what you already know about the topic, the questions you have, and any other thoughts or associations that come to mind. Remember, when you freewrite, you don't have to write in complete sentences. Just stay focused on the limited topic, and write down—as fast as you can—all the thoughts, images, questions, and ideas that occur to you. If you are freewriting on a computer, print out what you have written, or save it and back it up.

Exercise 7   **Making a KWL Chart**

Choose a different limited topic, and make a KWL chart like the one shown on page 16. (You can create the chart on paper or on a computer.) Fill in the topic and the first two columns (What I Already **K**now, What I **W**ant to Know). Save your chart so that you can complete the third column (What I **L**earned) after you've done your research.

Exercise 8 | **Revising Inappropriate Topics**

Tell why each topic below is inappropriate for a research paper. Then suggest two alternative but related topics for each. Keep in mind the four requirements for a workable topic. (See pages 11–12.) For example:

Inappropriate. Snowboarding (too general)

Workable. Dangers of snowboarding; comparing and contrasting water-skiing and snowboarding

1. My favorite Mexican foods

   _____

   _____

2. Space exploration in the year 2050

   _____

   _____

3. Airport security

   _____

   _____

4. Native American art

   _____

   _____

5. Grammy awards

   _____

   _____

6. Hurricanes

   _____

   _____

7. William Shakespeare's plays

   _____

   _____

8. Slang in my grandparents' day

   _____

   _____

9. Chinese immigration to the United States

_____

_____

10. Solar energy

_____

_____

Exercise 9 **Wording Your Research Questions**

On a separate sheet of paper or your computer, write several research questions for the limited topic that most interests you. These should simply be questions to which you would like to find the answers.

Exercise 10 **Checking Your Progress**

Answer each of the following questions about the work you've done so far.

1. What is the limited topic you have chosen to write about?

_____

_____

2. Are you satisfied with your research questions? Which one(s) appeal to you most? Why?

_____

_____

3. What other topic ideas did you seriously consider? (Write your second and third choices.)

_____

_____

4. How or where did you get the idea for your limited topic?

_____

_____

5. Which approaches to finding and limiting your topic did you try?

_____

_____

6. Which approaches did you think were most useful? Why?

_____

_____

Checklist Review

Monday 1 Are you on schedule?
Check the Timetables on page 10.

☐ Make sure you understand your assignment.

☐ Draw up a project schedule.

☐ Choose a workable topic that meets all of these requirements for a research paper topic:

- You can find enough material on the topic.
- The topic interests you, and you think you can make it interest your audience.
- The topic is objective, not subjective (if you are writing an informational, or factual, research paper).
- The topic is limited enough to be covered adequately in the space available.

☐ Word your limited topic as a research question that you are going to investigate.

STEP 2

For more on locating sources, see Step 2 in the two model research papers at **www.sadlierresearchpaper.com**.

Locate Sources

It is now time to locate sources of information you will need for your research paper. In this step, you will learn about the many resources available to you and how best to use them. Before starting out on Step 2, however, take a moment to check your progress against the timetable you have chosen as a model (see page 10). Remember, it's important to stay on schedule. Time lost or wasted now will be difficult—maybe impossible—to make up later.

Two Kinds of Sources

As you begin to look for information about your topic, you will explore two kinds of sources. A **primary source** is an original text, document, interview, speech, or letter. It is not someone's comments on or analysis of a text; it is the text itself. A **secondary source** is *not* an original text or document; rather, it is someone's comments on or analysis of a primary source. For example, U.S. census data are a primary source; a study of economic trends based on census data would be a secondary source.

Here are some examples of primary and secondary sources:

PRIMARY SOURCES: Literary works (poems, short stories, novels, essays, plays); documents; autobiographies; letters; interviews; speeches; surveys; tables of statistics

SECONDARY SOURCES: Comments on or analysis (either written or spoken) of an original text or document; biographies

Hint!

Try to include at least one primary source in your paper. Your comments on a primary source will show your knowledge about your topic. Primary sources also provide a welcome change from reading about other people's ideas and opinions.

☑ Evaluate the sources that you find.

CHECK THE DATE. You will want accurate, up-to-date information, especially if the topic involves the sciences or social sciences. An article published in 1978 about space stations is seriously out of date, but a 1978 article about William Shakespeare could still be an excellent source. You will have to look at the article to see.

CHECK THE AUTHOR. Is the writer an expert on the topic? You can usually find some information about the writer (educational and career background) on a book's title page or jacket or at the beginning or end of a magazine article. Is there any indication that the writer is biased or unreliable? You need to be especially careful about using information you find on the Internet. (See pages 26–27 on evaluating Internet sources.)

Library/Media Center Resources

Libraries are often called **media centers** these days, and librarians are **media specialists**. That is because most libraries offer videos, audiobooks, music CDs, movie DVDs, computer software, and electronic databases in addition to books, magazines, and newspapers.

☑ Start by exploring library resources.

Remember that you need five or more good sources (or whatever number your teacher has specified), so allow yourself plenty of time to adjust your topic as you turn up new information or run into dead ends. Some sources may be dated; others may be unavailable; some may turn out not to contain any useful information.

USE THE ONLINE CATALOG TO LOCATE BOOKS IN THE LIBRARY. The library's user-friendly computer catalog lets you search for books by author, title, and subject. You might also be able to conduct a **Boolean search**, a title search based on key words. After you enter two or more key words, the computer displays all the book titles containing those key words. Don't hesitate to ask your librarian for help.

When you look up a book in the library's catalog, you will find its **call number**, the series of numbers and letters printed on the book's spine. A call number is like a

---

Online Research There are a number of ways to get the most out of a Boolean search. In most cases, you can pull up titles with variants of key words by using the $ symbol. For example, to find myths about floods in cultures around the world, you might type these key words: *myth$* and *flood$*. The abbreviations *au.* and *ti.*, which stand for *author* and *title,* are also useful. For example, if you want to search for books about Willa Cather's *My Ántonia*, you would enter these key words: *cather.au.* and *my antonia.ti.*

---

road map; it tells you exactly where to find the book you are looking for. Call numbers come from either the **Dewey decimal system** or the **Library of Congress system** for classifying books by their subject. It is not necessary to memorize either system, but you do need to know that the call number of a nonfiction book indicates its general and specific subject and its author's last name. Nonfiction books are shelved according to their call numbers; books of fiction are shelved in a separate section, alphabetically by the author's last name.

USE THE REFERENCE SECTION TO FIND INFORMATION AND SOURCES. The library's reference section contains books and other materials that cannot be checked out. Here are some of the types of resources you can use:

Encyclopedias. Look up your topic in one or more of the standard multivolume encyclopedias, such as *World Book Encyclopedia*, *Encyclopedia Americana*, and *Encyclopaedia Britannica*. Your teacher may not accept encyclopedia articles as sources because they are too broad and general, but they will give you an overview of your topic. Also, at the end of many articles, you will find useful bibliographies— that is, lists of recommended books about the topic. Besides general encyclopedias, you may also find encyclopedias devoted to a single subject, such as the three-volume *Storytelling: An Encyclopedia of Mythology and Folklore*.

Biographical information. If you are tracking down information about a person, the reference section has many multivolume sources (such as *Contemporary Authors*). Some are published annually (such as *Who's Who in America*) or monthly (*Current Biography*). You will also find specialized biographical sources (such as *Notable Native Americans*, *Who's Who Among African Americans*, and *Who's Who in Animated Cartoons*).

Atlases. These oversized books contain maps as well as geographical and economic information. There are historical atlases that show past boundaries and current atlases that show nations, cities, and geographic features.

Almanacs. These single-volume books, published each year, are crammed with facts, charts, statistics, and other information.

Dictionaries. A reference section usually has one or more unabridged dictionaries—the oversized ones that contain nearly every word in the English language. There are specialized dictionaries, too, such as dictionaries of slang, sports terms, science, art, and foreign languages.

Quotations. Who said what, and when did he or she say it? If you are trying to track down the source of a familiar phrase or quotation, or if you are looking for a quotation on a specific topic, you will find an assortment of books, such as *Bartlett's Familiar Quotations*.

Specialized books on all subjects. The reference shelves are filled with many other books that librarians consider useful for research. You will find books about art history, science, math, and many other subjects. You will also find specialized indexes, such as *Book Review Digest*, *The Columbia Granger's Index to Poetry in Anthologies*, and *Humanities Index*.

USE ELECTRONIC DATABASES. Most school and public libraries subscribe to a variety of databases, which you can access on a computer at the library or sometimes at home. To use these electronic sources at home, you'll need a valid public library card. If you live near a college or university, you are usually welcome to use the library, where you will find even more electronic databases. You can read the full text of articles and then print (usually for a small fee) those that are relevant to your topic.

☑ **Ask a librarian at the reference desk for help in using electronic sources.**

You start at the library's home page, where you are given a list of choices. If you choose "Research Resources," you can access several dozen reliable electronic databases available to library patrons. A sampling of the sources that you are likely to find useful follows. All of these sites are searchable.

- **InfoTrac General OneFile** You'll be able to browse articles from more than 8,000 periodicals (journals, magazines, and newspapers).

- **Access World News** This source gives full-text articles from more than 1,500 U.S. and international newspapers, news magazines, news wire services (such as the Associated Press and Reuters), video news clips, and radio-broadcast transcripts.

- *The New York Times* Search the daily *New York Times* from 1851 to the present. Your library may have other national daily and regional weekly newspapers in its electronic databases.

- **Literature Criticism Online** You'll find articles on authors and literary works from the Middle Ages to the present in multivolume encyclopedias, such as *Twentieth-Century Literary Criticism, Short Story Criticism,* and *Poetry Criticism.*

- **Science Reference Center** This database gives full-text articles on science and technology, drawn from more than 600 encyclopedias, periodicals, and reference books. You can search a topic and ask for articles with a grade-level-appropriate Lexile score (reading level).

- **Online Reference Books** At one time, you had to go to the library to thumb through encyclopedias in person. Now you can sit at home and access full-text articles and images from digitized encyclopedias and specialized reference books. For example, you can read about the Florida Snail Kite, a hawk, in a 6-volume E-book called *Beacham's Guide to the Endangered Species of North America.*

- **Biography Resource Center** This source indexes biographies of more than 320,000 people from all over the world, past and present. This database also indexes magazine and newspaper articles and Web sites about these individuals. Articles are searchable by a person's name and by category, such as Nobel Prize winners, scientists, or world leaders.

- **History Reference Center** This source gives full-text articles from more than 650 historical reference sources (documents, biographies, encyclopedias, and reference books), covering U.S. and world history, from prehistory to the present.

Evaluating Internet Sources

USING SEARCH ENGINES. Search engines don't index exactly the same sites, so if you want a "second opinion"—because results do vary—try using more than one search engine. To narrow your search, start by condensing your topic into a few essential words, or enclose a phrase in double quotation marks.

☑ **Evaluate Internet sources carefully.**

Ask yourself these questions about information you discover on the Internet.

- **Who wrote the Web page?** Usually, you can find the name of the writer or organization (and sometimes an e-mail address) somewhere on the home page. How qualified or knowledgeable is the writer? Is the writer an expert or a professional working in the area the Web site discusses?

- **How accurate is the information?** Does the Web page give facts or just the writer's opinions? Verify factual information by locating the same facts in reliable print sources, such as encyclopedias or almanacs.

- **How up-to-date is the information?** Check the date on which the Web site was created and/or last updated.

- **Is the information biased (slanted toward one point of view), or are both sides of an issue presented objectively and fairly?** Bias is difficult to detect unless you know a lot about the topic or issue. Exaggeration, name-calling, and stereotyping are sure clues that the site is biased.

Checking the facts. Most publishers employ **fact-checkers** to double-check the facts in manuscripts submitted by authors, and they're not satisfied until they verify information with at least two reliable sources. But when you're looking at a Web site you've found through a search engine, you are totally on your own. Often, you have no idea who wrote the Web page or how reliable the information is.

Warning! A statement may sound like a fact, but that doesn't mean it is true. It may be an opinion, or it may contain false information. Consider this example: "Shakespeare's plays were actually written by Sir Francis Bacon." Is this statement a fact that can be proven to be true, or is it an opinion? If you check several reliable sources (such as *Encyclopaedia Britannica*'s entries on Shakespeare and Sir Francis Bacon, and an introduction to Shakespeare's plays written by a scholar), you will conclude that this factual-sounding statement is somebody's opinion, not a fact.

A useful indicator of a Web site's reliability is its **URL** (uniform or universal resource locater), or **Web address**. Here are some general guidelines:

Online Research

When evaluating an Internet source, look for these **top-level domains** in the address.

- **.gov** indicates that the information is posted by a government agency or group. Agencies such as the U.S. Census Bureau <http://www.census.gov> and the Department of Labor <http://www.dol.gov> publish detailed statistics that are generally reliable.

- **.edu** is an educational source. A Web site with an *.edu* domain was most likely created by someone associated with a college or university. A scholarly project at a university is almost always reliable.

- **.org** is a nonprofit organization. The Web page of a museum should be reliable, but look for bias in an organization sponsoring a cause.

- **.com** is usually a business. Since almost any person or organization can pay for a domain name, you should be wary of information from businesses that are trying to sell you a product or an entity that may have a hidden agenda. Most major news organizations have reliable sites, such as <http://www.washingtonpost.com> and <http://www.cnn.com>.

- **.net** indicates a variety of organizations that offer Internet services.

Exercise 1 Be a Fact-Checker

Suppose that you are a fact-checker for a publisher. How would you go about checking the following statements? On a separate piece of paper, write whether each item is a fact (**F**) or an opinion (**O**). Then, write at least two reliable sources you can use to verify or disprove each statement.

1. Chocolate is made from the fermented, dried beans found in the ripe pods of the cacao tree.
2. The U.S. Civil War ended when General Robert E. Lee surrendered to General Ulysses S. Grant at Appomattox Court House on April 9, 1865.
3. Mary Cassatt, an American Impressionist painter, was born in Philadelphia in 1834 but lived much of her life in Europe.
4. Scholars agree that America's greatest president was Abraham Lincoln.
5. The first collection of Emily Dickinson's poetry appeared in 1890 and was edited by Mabel Loomis Todd and T.W. Higgins, who made many changes from Dickinson's original punctuation and wording.
6. Faith Ringgold (1930–) is a successful African American artist best known for her story quilts.
7. In 1519, the Spanish Conquistadores led by Hernán Cortés laid siege and then destroyed the beautiful Aztec capital of Tenochtitlan, which was rebuilt as Mexico City.

WORKING TOGETHER | **Exercise 2** **Evaluating Search Engine Results**

Choose two of the following topics, and use two different search engines to find information about them. Work with a partner to create search terms that will pull up fewer hits. Without looking at the actual Web sites, decide which sites you think will be the most reliable. Explain why.

1. how to cure hiccups
2. Michelangelo and the ceiling of the Sistine Chapel in the Vatican, Italy
3. Jason and the Golden Fleece
4. the origins of the sport of basketball
5. Theodore Roosevelt and the formation of the National Park system
6. the volcanic eruption of Mt. St. Helens in southwest Washington in 1980
7. the first walk on the moon, July 21, 1969
8. the proposed Equal Rights Amendment to the U.S. Constitution
9. E. B. White's success as a children's book author
10. the Beatles' first trip to the United States

WORKING TOGETHER | **Exercise 3** **Evaluating Web Sites**

Work with a partner. Rank each of these Web sites from 1 (lowest) to 4 (highest) according to how reliable and accurate you think the information on the Web site will be. Be prepared to explain your evaluation.

1. the most recent U.S. Department of Labor statistics on the number of women in the workforce
2. a twelfth-grader's blog entry about the early history of silent movies
3. the Public Broadcasting Service's (PBS) timeline on the life of African American writer and poet Langston Hughes
4. an editorial about Abraham Lincoln, from the *New York Times*, January 1862
5. a Wikipedia article about a controversial political issue
6. an article by an unknown writer about the Battle of Hastings (1066) on a Web site called www.battle1066.com
7. an article about Cushing's disease, a serious illness that affects dogs, by a dog trainer
8. an eighth grader's science report on solar wind farms, published on her school's Web site
9. the transcript of *Brown v. Board of Education* from the U.S. Supreme Court
10. a brief biography of Pablo Picasso from an art gallery

Exercise 4 **Where Would You Look?**

For each of the research questions listed below, write at least one sentence telling how you would look up information about the topic. (Use a separate sheet of paper or your computer.) What sources would you explore?

1. What are the latest research findings on the effects of dopamine, a chemical that transmits signals in the brain?
2. How do weather forecasters track and predict the force of hurricanes?
3. What is the history of Key West, the southernmost city in the continental United States?
4. What are some of the latest ideas on how to increase voter turnout?
5. How was the polio epidemic in the United States stopped?
6. What is the story behind Shackleton's 1914–1916 voyage to Antarctica?
7. What is the history of breakthrough motion picture inventions such as sound, color, the blue screen, and animation?
8. What are the major themes of the Mesopotamian epic *Gilgamesh*?
9. What does Picasso's painting *Guernica* represent?
10. What factors led to the extinction of the passenger pigeon?

Exercise 5 **Evaluating Internet Sources**

For each numbered item, choose the Web site that you predict will be most relevant and reliable. Be prepared to explain why you made your choice.

1. For a research paper on the history of the sport of lacrosse:
   a. www.lacrosse.com (home page of Great Atlantic Lacrosse Company, which sells lacrosse equipment)
   b. www.lacrosse.org (the home page of US Lacrosse, the governing body of men's and women's lacrosse teams in the United States)
   c. www.lacrosseuniversity.com (Web site of Lacrosse University in Bay St. Louis, MS)
   d. www.warriorlacrosse.com (Web site of a manufacturer of lacrosse equipment and clothing)

2. For a research paper on Ansel Adams's photographs in Yosemite National Park:
   a. www.nps.gov/yose/nature/articles/adams.htm (Yosemite National Park Web site article about Adams's special relationship with Yosemite)
   b. www.quotationspage.com/quotes/Ansel_Adams (quotations by Ansel Adams)
   c. www.anseladams.com (Web site of Ansel Adams Gallery, which sells photos, posters, books; several pages of biography; bibliography)
   d. www.ncsu.edu/project/farkas/yosemite.html (Adams's photograph of El Capitan and Half Dome, with a very brief quotation by Adams)

Exercise 6 Getting Started

As you start gathering information for your report, brainstorm a list of library and computer resources that you might explore. (Use a separate sheet of paper or your computer.) Visit the library and start tracking down these sources, adding to your list as you research further. Next to each item on your list, note very briefly those sources that seem useful, those that do not, and why.

Community Resources

☑ **Find primary sources by exploring community resources.**

Libraries and computers are not the only sources of information. Check out sources in your own community. Who knows a lot about or has had experience related to your topic? Where can you go to find information related to your topic? What questions would you ask an expert? You will create original **primary sources** as you write letters and conduct interviews and surveys.

WRITE TO AN EXPERT. If your topic is the migration pattern of monarch butterflies, you might write to a professor of entomology (the science of studying insects) at a local college or to a local resident who has a large butterfly collection.

Follow these guidelines when you write letters or e-mails asking for information:

- Find out the person's name, title, and address, and follow the proper form for a business letter.
- Write your letter or e-mail as soon as you can so that you allow enough time for a reply. (The problem with gathering information by writing letters is that you have no control over how quickly you will receive a reply.)
- Be polite, and ask specific questions that show you already have some knowledge of your topic.
- If you receive a reply, write a short note thanking the person for the information you've received.

Exercise 7 Writing a Letter or E-Mail

Write to someone who might provide you with information on the topic you have chosen for your report. Find the name of the person, the person's complete address (including the zip code), and write the letter. (The address can be omitted from an E-mail.) You do not have to restrict yourself to people in your community; you can write to anyone who might have personal knowledge about your topic. Be sure to follow the proper form for a business letter. You might use the model letter shown on page 31.

13001 Marigold Lane
Silver Spring, MD 20906

April 19, 2009

Ms. Selma Owens, Director of Communications
Maryland Youth Lacrosse League
8010 Loch Raven Boulevard
Towson, MD 21285

Dear Ms. Owens:

I am a 9th grade student at John F. Kennedy High School. I am writing a research paper on lacrosse and am especially interested in Youth Lacrosse. Can you please tell me about the history of Youth Lacrosse in the United States?

I would also like to know what a school has to do in order to start a lacrosse team. If you have any publications that describe the rules and regulations of Youth Lacrosse, I would really appreciate your sending this information to me.

Thank you for your help. I look forward to hearing from you.

Sincerely,

Benjamin Spragg

Benjamin Spragg

CONDUCT AN INTERVIEW IN PERSON OR ON THE TELEPHONE OR INTERNET. Instead of writing letters to ask questions, you might call or write someone knowledgeable about your topic to arrange for an interview. Interviews are particularly important if you are writing an I-Search research paper. Follow these important steps:

- Before you get started, make sure that you have your teacher's permission for the interview.
- Either by letter or phone, explain to the interviewee who you are, what you are writing about, and why you think he or she might be helpful.

- Ask for a limited amount of time, perhaps 20–30 minutes, and set a definite day and time for the interview.

- Before the interview, prepare five to ten clearly worded questions that will yield specific information and guide the interview. Keep in mind that a prepared question may bring a reply that leads to other questions and answers. It is important to remain flexible enough to pursue unexpected leads.

- Appear (or call) promptly for the interview. Be polite and take notes. If you are going to record the interview, ask for permission in advance.

- Ask for permission to use direct quotes from the interview in your paper.

- Don't overstay your welcome. Thank the person for his or her time, and send a follow-up letter of thanks.

WORKING TOGETHER   **Exercise 8**   **Preparing for an Interview**

Draft five questions you would ask each of the following persons in an interview on the topic given. Phrase your questions in a way that will encourage the person you are interviewing to respond with specific details. You might work with a partner to test your questions.

1. A famous sports figure (name him or her) on how to prepare for a career in his or her field

Name of person: _____

_____

_____

_____

_____

_____

2. A local government official on juvenile crime (or any other serious issue) in your community

Name of person: _____

_____

_____

_____

_____

_____

_____

3. Your school principal (or a school board member or the superintendent of schools) on an education issue (curriculum, safety, testing, class size, educational reform, vocational education, dropouts, etc.)

Name of person: _____

_____

_____

_____

_____

VISIT A LOCAL MUSEUM OR GOVERNMENT OFFICE. You might sit in on a city council meeting or visit a local recycling plant. Is there a nearby museum related to your topic, where you might find exactly the information you need for your report? Check with the librarian or curator at the museum for help in tracking down the information you need. If you visit a government office, request publications or other information from a receptionist, who will direct you to the proper person or office.

Exercise 9   Focusing on Your Community

On a separate sheet of paper or your computer, write a few sentences for each of the research questions below, telling where and how you would find information in your community. List specific names and addresses if possible.

1. What organized after-school athletic programs are available for elementary school boys and girls in your community?
2. What is your community doing or planning to do about recycling? How successful have recycling projects been during the last three years?
3. What specific resources does the community provide for senior citizens? What needs are not being met? How might the community meet these needs?
4. What is the procedure for deciding how local taxes are spent? What were last year's expenditures, and what is the proposed budget for the coming year?
5. What local organizations are available for people interested in the arts? Are there music groups, theater groups, book groups?
6. Who are the current members of the local school board, and how are they elected? How are changes in school policy decided?
7. How many law enforcement officers are there in your community? What training do they undergo before they join the force?
8. Who are your elected representatives in the state legislature? Who are your elected representatives in Congress? How can you reach each of them?
9. What are the most recent statistics on crime in your community? Are serious crimes on the rise, or are they declining?
10. What percentage of the ninth grade class in your school goes on to graduate from high school? What percentage of the high school graduates goes on to college?

CONDUCT A SURVEY. When you conduct a survey, you have a chance to ask people everything you want to know about your topic. First, you will have to figure out a useful **sampling**, the group of people you will ask to complete your **questionnaire**. Then you will have to write clearly worded questions designed to elicit the information you are looking for. Instead of providing blank lines and asking people to write in their own answers to your questions, give them a choice of responses. This will make it easier to tally the results.

Here is an example of a survey question and a choice of responses:

EXAMPLE

```
How many hours of television do you watch on an average
weekday during the school year? (Include both daytime and
evening viewing.)
    ❑ none          ❑ less than 1     ❑ 1–2 hours
    ❑ 2–3 hours     ❑ 3–5 hours       ❑ 6 or more hours
```

Creating a survey or questionnaire takes careful planning. Consider all the following questions:

- Who will be included in your sampling group, and how many people will you survey? (The larger and more random the sample, the more accurate or representative your information will be. For example, instead of surveying just your close friends, you will get a more random sampling by surveying every other person in three or four homerooms at different grade levels.)

- How can you ensure that you will get enough responses?

- Whose permission will you need to distribute your questionnaire?

- What specific information do you want to find?

- Are your questions clearly worded? (You might try out your survey on several friends.)

- Are the responses designed so that they can be tallied easily?

- What conclusions can you make based on the results of your survey?

 WORKING TOGETHER **Exercise 10** **Conducting a Survey**

Pretend that as part of your research paper on the TV-watching habits of students, you are going to conduct a survey. On a separate sheet of paper or your computer, draft at least six questions with responses that can be tallied easily. Compare your questions with those of your classmates. You might create a class questionnaire and distribute it to other English classes. Tally the results, and decide what you can conclude from the survey.

Exercise 11 Getting Started

On a separate sheet of paper or your computer, name one **primary source** that you plan to explore for your research paper: a letter, an interview, a visit, a survey. Detail the steps you will use, and compose whatever needs to be written.

a. **Letter.** If you are writing a letter asking for information, find out the name, title, and address of a person who might provide the information. Draft the letter, revise it, and send it. Report to a classmate or classmates on the reply you receive.

b. **Interview.** Find out the name of a person you might interview. Draft ten questions you would ask that person. (Be sure to word your questions so that you get more than a *yes* or *no* answer.) Choose your best questions (at least six), and call or write to arrange for an interview. Be sure your teacher approves your interview plans.

c. **Visit.** Determine if there is a local museum or government office that might have information that you need on your topic. Find out the location and hours when you can visit. Plan your visit, and write down the information you gather.

d. **Survey.** Think of a survey that might help you gather useful information for your report. Who would take the survey? Draft a questionnaire (at least seven or eight questions with responses), revise it, and distribute it to your sample. Tally your results, and decide what conclusions you can draw.

Working Bibliography: Keeping Track of Sources

☑ **Record complete information for every source you think you will use.**

When you write your final research paper, you must tell the reader where you got your information. That's why you need to create a **working bibliography** to keep careful track of your sources. Your working bibliography may either be on 3" x 5" or 4" x 6" index cards, or you can create a separate computer file that lists every source you consult. For each source, record the author, title, and publishing information (place of publication, publisher, and date of publication). If you are using an electronic source, you will also need to write the date on which you accessed the information and, if it's an Internet source, the URL (the Web address—e.g., http://www.cnn.com).

Assign each source a number, and write it in the upper right-hand corner of the index card or at the top of each entry in your computer file. When you start taking notes from that source, write the source number on any additional note cards; this allows you to keep track of where your notes came from, without having to repeatedly write the same source information on the additional cards. If you want, you might also add your own note or comment about the source, as shown in the two examples on the next page.

Book

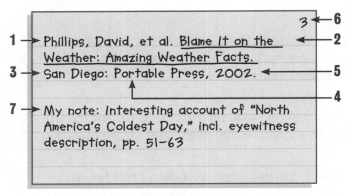

1 Author(s) or editor(s), last name first
2 Book's title, underlined
3 Place of publication
4 Publisher
5 Date of publication
6 Researcher's source number
7 Researcher's comment

Newspaper or Magazine Article

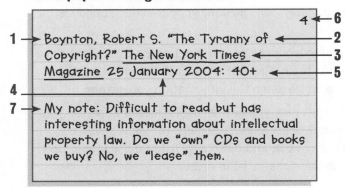

1 Author(s), if given
2 Article's title, enclosed in quotation marks
3 Newspaper's or magazine's title, underlined
4 Date of publication
5 Page(s) on which article appears
6 Researcher's source number
7 Researcher's comment

☑ Write each bibliography entry according to the style your teacher requires.

You will follow the exact same style when you write the entries for your Works Cited list, so getting the entries in the correct format now will save you a lot of time later. In the sample bibliography cards above and in the entries on pages 37–42, pay special attention to three things:

- the information that is given

- the order in which the information is given

- the punctuation of each item

The entries in this book follow the **MLA (Modern Language Association)** style for documenting sources, which is the style most often required by high school and college teachers. (For the **APA [American Psychological Association]** style, see Appendix C.) Whatever style of documentation your teacher requires, be sure to follow it exactly.

The following pages show examples of the MLA style for documenting sources. Unless your teacher directs you to use a different style, this is the style you will use to prepare your **Works Cited list** or **bibliography** (see Step 7). Each example shows the necessary information, the order in which it is given, and the proper punctuation. In every entry in a Works Cited list, indent turnover lines.

MLA Style of Documenting Sources

Note: MLA Style now requires that you identify the type of source from which you obtained your information—e.g., Print, Web, E-mail, CD-ROM, Audiocassette.

 Books

BOOK BY A SINGLE AUTHOR

Torre, Joe. *The Yankee Years*. New York: Doubleday, 2009. Print.

TWO OR MORE BOOKS BY THE SAME AUTHOR

After the first mention of an author's name, use three hyphens followed by a period to indicate "same author as above."

Austen, Jane. *Northanger Abbey*. Ed. Anne Henry Ehrenpreis. London: Penguin, 1985. Print.

---. *Persuasion*. Ed. D. W. Harding. London: Penguin, 1985. Print.

BOOK BY TWO AUTHORS

Cosby, Camille O., and Renee Poussaint. *A Wealth of Wisdom: Legendary African American Elders Speak*. New York: Atria, 2004. Print.

BOOK BY FOUR OR MORE AUTHORS

List only the first author followed by the abbreviation *et al.* ("and others").

Greenough, Sarah, et al. *On the Art of Fixing a Shadow: One Hundred and Fifty Years of Photography*. Washington, DC: National Gallery of Art, 1989. Print.

BOOK BY A SINGLE EDITOR

Kennedy, Caroline, ed. *A Patriot's Handbook: Songs, Poems, Stories, and Speeches Celebrating the Land We Love*. New York: Hyperion, 2003. Print.

BOOK BY SINGLE AUTHOR WITH EDITORS AND TRANSLATOR

Frank, Anne. *The Diary of a Young Girl: Definitive Edition*. Eds. Otto H. Frank and Mirjam Pressler. Trans. Susan Massotty. New York: Doubleday, 1995. Print.

BOOK BY TWO EDITORS

Goldhammer, Arthur, and Christine Klapish-Zuber, eds. *A History of Women in the West, Vol. 2: Silences of the Middle Ages*. Cambridge, MA: Belknap, 1994. Print.

BOOK BY THREE OR MORE EDITORS

Appiah, Kwame Anthony, et al., eds. *The Dictionary of Global Culture*. New York: Knopf, 1996. Print.

Perkins, George, Barbara Perkins, and Phillip Leininger, eds. *Benét's Reader's Encyclopedia of American Literature*. New York: Harper, 1991. Print.

BOOK WITH NO AUTHOR CITED

The Baseball Encyclopedia. 9th ed. New York: Macmillan, 1993. Print.

BOOK THAT IS PART OF A SERIES

Soumerai, Eva Nussbaum, and Carol D. Schulz. *A Voice from the Holocaust*. Westport, CT: Greenwood, 2003. Print. Voices of Twentieth-Century Conflict Ser.

MULTIVOLUME WORK

Hunter, Jeffrey W., et al., eds. *Contemporary Literary Criticism*. Vol. 148. Farmington Hills, MI: Gale, 2002. Print.

EDITION

Lincoln, C. Eric. *The Black Muslims in America*. 3rd ed. Trenton, NJ: Africa World, 1994. Print.

TRANSLATION

Appelfeld, Aharon. *To the Land of the Cattails*. Trans. Jeffrey M. Green. New York: Grove, 1994. Print.

GOVERNMENT PUBLICATION

United States. U.S. General Accounting Office. *Student Testing: Current Extent and Expenditures, with Cost Estimates for a National Examination*. Washington, DC: GAO, 1993. Print.

PAMPHLET

Stevenson, George B. *Trees of Everglades National Park and the Florida Keys*. 2nd ed. Miami: Banyan, 1969. Print.

☑ Parts of Books

STORY, ESSAY, POEM, OR PLAY IN A BOOK BY A SINGLE AUTHOR

Erdrich, Louise. "Indian Boarding School: The Runaways." *Original Fire: Selected and New Poems*. New York: Harper, 2003. Print.

STORY, ESSAY, POEM, OR PLAY IN AN ANTHOLOGY

García Márquez, Gabriel. "A Very Old Man with Enormous Wings." Trans. Gregory Rabassa. *Collected Stories*. New York: Harper, 1984. 203–10. Print.

Hurston, Zora Neal. "Drenched in Light." *The Portable Harlem Renaissance Reader*. Ed. David Levering Lewis. New York: Viking, 1994. 691–98. Print.

INTRODUCTION, FOREWORD, OR PREFACE
By the author of the work

Porter, Katherine Anne. "Go Little Book . . ." Preface. *The Collected Stories of Katherine Anne Porter*. New York: Harcourt, 1965. v–vi. Print.

By someone other than the author of a work

Baldwin, James. "Sweet Lorraine." Introduction. *To Be Young, Gifted and Black*. By Lorraine Hansberry, adapted by Robert Nemiroff. Englewood Cliffs, NJ: Prentice Hall, 1969. ix–xii. Print.

ARTICLE IN AN ENCYCLOPEDIA OR OTHER REFERENCE BOOK
Unsigned

For a familiar reference work, you do not have to cite the city and publisher. Articles from less familiar reference books should have full publishing information (place of publication and publisher).

"Islamic Art and Architecture." *The Columbia Encyclopedia*. 6th ed. 2001. Print.

"Dominican Republic." *Statesman's Year-Book, 1995–96*. 132nd ed. Ed. Brian Hunter. New York: St. Martin's, 1995. 492–96. Print.

Signed

Wiggins, David K. "Jesse Owens." *The Oxford Companion to United States History*. New York: Oxford, 2001. Print.

☑ Magazine and Newspaper Articles
MAGAZINE ARTICLE

Notice how the date (day of month followed by abbreviated month) and page numbers are cited. Do not cite volume or issue numbers. A plus sign (+) indicates that the article begins on that page and is continued on the following pages, which are not consecutive.

Kingsolver, Barbara. "What Money Doesn't Buy: Microfinance and Women's Empowerment in South Asia." *World Ark* Mar./Apr. 2009: 12+. Print.

NEWSPAPER ARTICLE

Taub, Erica A. "Webcam Brings 3-D to Topps Sports Cards." *New York Times* 9 Mar. 2009, Southern ed. B4. Print.

NEWSPAPER EDITORIAL

"Voting Rights Progress." Editorial. *Wall Street Journal* 10 Mar. 2009: A14. Print.

NEWSPAPER COLUMN

Geithner, Timothy, and Shaun Donovan. "Housing Plan's Aim: Help People Help Themselves." *USA Today* 19 Feb. 2009: 9A. Print.

Whitney, Meredith. "Credit Cards Are the Next Credit Crunch." *Wall Street Journal* 10 Mar. 2009: A15. Print.

LETTER TO THE EDITOR

Johnson, Shirley. Letter. *Palm Beach Post* 6 Mar. 2009: A12. Print.

☑ Electronic Sources

In addition to electronic publication information, you must include the date you accessed the site, which is the second date given in the following examples. At one time, writers were also required to cite the full URL (web address) for any source found on the Internet. MLA style no longer requires URLs for several reasons: (1) Web sites change frequently as they are updated, (2) Web sites sometimes disappear altogether, and (3) the URLs are often so long that errors occur when you try to record them. According to the latest *MLA Handbook,* the Works Cited list should include a URL only if you think it will be too difficult to find the Web site without the URL.

Your teacher may still prefer that you include all of the URLs on your Works Cited list. Therefore, some of the following examples contain URLs to show you what they should look like and where to place them. **Note:** All electronic sources should be identified with the word *Web,* which is placed immediately before the date on which you accessed the Web site.

ONLINE MAGAZINE ARTICLE
Landsburg, Steven E. "Grade Expectations." *Slate* 12 Aug. 1999. Web. 12 Jan. 2008. <http://slate.msn.com/id/33044>.

ONLINE NEWSPAPER ARTICLE
Associated Press. "Freeing Willy, in Real Life." *New York Times on the Web* 8 Sept. 1999. Web. 22 Dec. 1999. <http://search.nytimes.com/>.

ONLINE REFERENCE WORK
Tufts, Eleanor. "Cassatt, Mary." *Grolier Multimedia Encyclopedia*. Scholastic, 2004. Web. 19 Sept. 2004. <http://gme.grolier.com>.

SCHOLARLY PROJECT
The Avalon Project. 1996–2003. Yale U. Law School. Web. 2 June 2003.

PROFESSIONAL WEB SITE
Willett, Perry, ed. *Victorian Women Writers Project*. Dec. 2000. Indiana U. Web. 3 Feb. 2003. <http://www.indiana.edu/~letrs/vwwp/>.

PAGE ON A WEB SITE
"Information Technology." *Career Voyages*. U.S. Departments of Labor and Education. 9 Feb. 2008. Web. 12 May 2010.

"NFL Standings: Division." *National Football League (NFL)*. 6 Mar. 2009. Web. 7 Mar. 2009. <http://www.nfl.com/standings>

Stolley, Karl, Kristen Seas, Tony Rouse, and Elizabeth Angeli. "MLA Formatting and Style Guide." *The OWL (Online Writing Lab) at Purdue*. 25 Feb. 2009. Purdue University Writing Lab. Web. 16 Oct. 2009.

"Where We Work: Around the World and in a Myriad of Habitats." *The Nature Conservancy*. 2009. Web. 14 Oct. 2009.

Entire book (e-book)

Mallegg, Kristen B., ed. *Who's Who Among African Americans*. Detroit: Gale, 2008. Web. 6 Jan. 2010.

Plotkin, David. *How to Do Everything with Photoshop Elements 3.0*. New York: McGraw Hill/Osborne, 2005. Web. 7 June 2010.

Image (photograph, work of art, sculpture) found online

Adams, Ansel. "Moonrise, Hernandez, New Mexico." 1941. "Ansel Anecdotes: Perspectives on Moonrise." Web. 8 Feb. 2010.

Cézanne, Paul. "The Artist's Father, Reading 'L'Événement.' " 1866. National Gallery of Art. Web. 5 May 2010.

"Oakland, California." Map. *U.S. Gazetteer*. U.S. Census Bureau. Web. 22 June 2009.

Weblog (blog) entries

Davidson, Jenny. "Nipped." Weblog entry. *Light Reading*. 1 Mar. 2009. Web. 5 Mar. 2009 <http://www.jennydavidson.blogspot.com>

Dusoulier, Clotilde. "Maple Pecan Ice Cream." Weblog entry. *Chocolate and Zucchini*. 25 Feb. 2009. Web. 25 July 2010.

Posting to a newsgroup or forum

Sussman, Mick. "'The Great Gatsby' by F. Scott Fitzgerald." Online posting. 1 Apr. 2002. 2003 Reading Group Archive. Web. 18 Mar. 2004.

E-mail

Hadley, Karen. "Re: Chocolate." Message to the author. 16 Sept. 2010. E-mail.

Ketchum, Robin. "Re: Summer plans for our trip on the Alaskan ferry." Message to Florence Valentino. 5 Dec. 2010. E-mail.

Online video

Murphy, Professor Kevin. "Robert Frost's 'The Road Not Taken.' " YouTube. Ithaca College, New York. Web. 6 Mar. 2009.

CD-ROM encyclopedia article

"Antarctica." *Complete Reference Collection*. Cambridge: The Learning Company, 1997. CD-ROM.

☑ Other Sources

Television or radio program

Nightly News with Brian Williams. NBC. WPTV-TV5. Boynton Beach, FL. 12 Feb. 2010. Television.

Sound recording (tape, CD, LP)

Tolkien, J. R. R. *The Fellowship of the Ring. The Lord of the Rings, Book One*. Narrated by Rob Inglis. Recorded Books, 2001. Audiocassettes.

FILM OR VIDEO RECORDING

Bram Stoker's Dracula. Dir. Francis Ford Coppola. Sony Pictures Home
    Entertainment. 2007. Film.

The Grapes of Wrath. Screenplay by Nunnally Johnson. Dir. John Ford. Perf. John
    Carradine, Jane Darwell, and Henry Fonda. Writ. Nunnally Johnson. Twentieth
    Century-Fox, 1940. Film.

PERFORMANCE (CONCERT, PLAY, OPERA, BALLET)

To Be Young, Gifted and Black. By Lorraine Hansberry. Dir. Gene Frankel.
    Perf. Barbara Baxley, Rita Gardner, Janet League, Cicely Tyson, John Beal,
    Gertrude Jeanette, Stephen Strimpell, Andre Womble. Cherry Lane Theatre,
    New York. 2 Jan. 1969. Performance.

WORK OF ART

Hopper, Edward. *Office in a Small City*. 1953. Oil on canvas. Metropolitan Museum
    of Art, New York.

INTERVIEW

Published interview

Drossos, George. Interview. *Division Street America*. By Studs Terkel. New York:
    Pantheon, 1967. 93–96. Print.

Unpublished interview

Santiago, Fabiola. Personal interview. 31 Jan. 2010.

LETTER

Published letter

Crane, Stephen. "To Joseph Conrad." 17 Mar. 1898. Letter 228 in *Stephen Crane:*
    Letters. Ed. R. W. Stallman and Lillian Gilkes. New York: New York UP, 1960.
    176–77. Print.

Unpublished letter

Angelou, Maya. Letter to the author. 6 Mar. 2003. TS.[1]

MAP OR CHART

Texas. Map. Chicago: Rand, 2000. Print.

CARTOON

Heller, Joe. "Twitter." Cartoon. *Green Bay Press-Gazette* 6 Mar. 2009: 24. Print.

Stavro/Lebanon. Cartoon. *Miami Herald* 2 Feb. 2004: 18A. Print.

LECTURE, SPEECH, OR ADDRESS

Faulkner, William. Stockholm, Sweden. 10 Dec. 1950. Nobel Prize speech.

Kennedy, John F. Washington, DC. 20 Jan. 1961. Inaugural address.

Obama, Barack. Washington, DC. 20 Jan. 2009. Inaugural address.

---

[1]*TS* stands for typescript; *MS* stands for manuscript.

Write a working bibliography entry (either on an index card or a computer file) for each of the following items. Use the MLA style shown on the preceding pages. Be sure to give the information in the proper order, and use the correct punctuation.

1. Tom Hooper is the director of the television miniseries *John Adams*, which was produced by HBO Video. All episodes of the series can be found on *John Adams*, three videodiscs (DVDs) that were released in 2008. You want to cite the DVDs.

2. You are citing an article on the history of Antarctica from Wikipedia, the free online encyclopedia. You accessed the article yesterday.

3. Barbara Damrosch is the author of a book titled *The Garden Primer*. It is the second edition and was published in 2008 by Workman Publishing Company in New York.

4. *Street Gang: The Complete History of Sesame Street* was written by Michael Davis. Viking publishing company published the book in 2008. Viking is located in New York.

5. On January 12, 2009, Terry Kurtz received an e-mail from Mayor Alice Segal. Mayor Segal was replying to Terry's earlier e-mail with questions about the city's plans for the proposed Youth Recreation Center.

6. You are using one page from a Web site in your research paper. The Web site is run by the National Park Service. The page you are using is titled "Internships." You accessed the page on December 19, 2009. The URL is <http://www.nps.gov/gettinginvolved/internships/index.htm>. Your teacher has asked you to include the URL in your entry.

7. Scott Adams is the author of a book of cartoons titled *Dilbert and the Way of the Weasel*. It was published in 2002. The publisher is HarperBusiness, which is located in New York.

8. Peter James and Nick Thorpe are the two editors of a book called *Ancient Inventions*. Their publisher is Ballantine Books in New York. The book appeared in 1999.

9. Jay Hyams is the translator and Giovanni [first name] Pinna is the author of a book about fossils. Its title is *The Illustrated Encyclopedia of Fossils*. It was published in 1990 by Facts on File in New York.

10. The author of a biography called *W. B. Yeats: A Life* is R. F. Foster. The biography is subtitled *Vol. II: The Arch-Poet (1915–1939)*. The book is published by Oxford University Press, which is located in Oxford, UK. It was published in 2003.

Exercise 13 | **What Is Wrong with These Working Bibliography Entries?**

Each of the following working bibliography entries contains at least one error; some contain many errors. Rewrite each entry, following exactly the MLA style as described on pages 37–42. Check carefully the punctuation, the information included, and the order in which the information is given.

1. YouTube video. Dr. Martin Luther King, Jr. "I Have a Dream." 28, Aug., 1963. 6 Oct. 2009. URL is http://www.youtube.com/watch?v=PbUtL_0vAJk

   _____

   _____

2. Lama, Dalai. *In My Own Words: An Introduction to my teachings and philosophy.* Hay House in Carlsbad, California, 2008

   _____

   _____

3. Carla Sanchez. Message to the author. E-mail. Jan. 26, 2010.

   _____

   _____

4. Friedman, Thomas L. *The World Is Flat.* Farrar, Straus & Giroux in 2006 in New York. Print.

   _____

   _____

5. Ralph Hickok. *A Who's Who of Sports Champions.* Houghton Mifflin, New York, 1995.

   _____

   _____

6. Editor, Jeff Silverman. Text by Lardner, Ring. *Lardner on Baseball.* 2002, Lyons Press in Guilford, CT.

   _____

   _____

7. Allende, Isabel. *Paula.* Translated by Margaret Sayers Peden. 1994, HarperCollins: New York.

   _____

   _____

8. Isaac Victor Kerlow. *The Art of 3D: Computer Animation and Effects, Third edition.* Hoboken, NJ, John Wiley & Sons. 2004. 3rd edition. Print.

   _____

   _____

9. Glanz, James, "Uut and Uup Add Their Atomic Mass to Periodic Table" in *New York Times*, a newspaper, February 1, 2004, page 1 southern edition, section YT.

_____

_____

10. Kennedy, Joseph. "The Wild Man of Samoa." *Natural History*, a magazine. Feb. 2004. Pages 22–25, 66. Print.

_____

_____

Exercise 14 Exploring Sources

On a separate sheet of paper or your computer, list every source that you explore as you do research for your paper. Follow exactly the MLA style for documenting sources, as shown on pages 37–42. Write a working bibliography entry for each source that you consult.

Exercise 15 Checking Your Progress

Answer each of the following questions about the work you've done so far.

1. Of the sources that you explored, which ones did you choose as the most relevant and reliable? Where did you find each of these sources?

_____

_____

2. How many bibliography source cards have you made so far? How many sources does your teacher require?

_____

_____

3. What community resources have you explored?

_____

_____

4. How did you judge which Internet sources are most reliable?

_____

_____

5. If you need to find more sources, where will you look?

_____

_____

Checklist Review

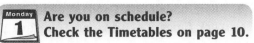 **Are you on schedule?**
Check the Timetables on page 10.

☐ Evaluate the sources that you find. Make sure they are relevant and reliable. Be especially careful when evaluating Internet sources.

☐ Start by exploring library resources.
- Use the online catalog to locate books in the library.
- Use the reference section to find information and sources.
- Use electronic databases.

☐ Ask a librarian at the reference desk for help in using electronic sources.
- Evaluate Internet sources carefully.

☐ Find primary sources by exploring community resources.
- Write a letter or an E-mail to an expert.
- Conduct an interview in person or on the telephone.
- Visit a local museum or government office.
- Conduct a survey.

☐ Record complete information for every source you think you will use.

☐ Write each bibliography entry according to the style your teacher requires.

For more on taking notes, see Step 3 in the two model research papers at www.sadlierresearchpaper.com.

STEP 3

Take Notes

BIG NATE reprinted by permission of United Features Syndicate, Inc.

Now that you have tracked down your sources, you are about to start the task of gathering information for your research paper. Note–taking is a crucial step on the way to your finished paper. If you do a good job taking notes, all the rest of the steps in completing your research paper will be a lot easier. But if you are careless—if, for example, you do not take care to record and credit your sources fully and accurately—you will make more work for yourself later on.

Working Outline

☑ **Before you start taking notes, create a working outline.**

Stop to make a plan, a road map to see where you are headed. Like all outlines, a working outline lists main topics and subtopics in some kind of logical order, but a working outline is informal and definitely not final. (You will make your final outline later.) Its purpose is to guide your research and note-taking. The following questions will help you plan your working outline.

- What are my research questions, the questions I want to find the answers to?
- What are the most important ideas I want to cover in my paper?
- What background information will readers need to have?
- What are the main parts, or sections, of my paper, and how do they relate to one another?
- How might I best organize the information?
- What conclusion(s) do I expect to draw?

You will probably revise your working outline several times as you take notes and think about your paper. You may decide to drop, add, change, or rearrange topics and subtopics as you discover, or are unable to find, the information that you are looking for.

Here is an example of a working outline for a paper about lacrosse:

```
                    Lacrosse: Yesterday and Today
  I. History of lacrosse
     A. Developed by Native Americans
        1. A violent game called "baggataway"
        2. Used to train warriors
     B. Adopted by French settlers in Canada
        1. Called lacrosse
        2. 1856—Montreal Lacrosse Club
        3. 1860—rules standardized
 II. How the game is played
     A. Teams
     B. Rules
     C. Equipment
III. Lacrosse today
     A. For both women and men
     B. In high schools
     C. In colleges
     D. International lacrosse
```

Exercise 1 — **Making a Working Outline for Your Paper**

On a separate sheet of paper or your computer, write a working outline for your research paper. Think about the main ideas you want to cover and how best to arrange them. Remember that you will probably revise this working outline as you continue to research and take notes.

☑ Skim your sources to locate information for your paper.

Skimming is the very fast type of reading you use when you search for specific information or for a particular kind of information.

Here's how to skim for information if your source is a book:

- Turn to the index (if there is one) at the back of the book or to the table of contents at the front. Look for headings related to your topic and research questions.

- When you find a heading that seems useful, turn to the page(s) listed and skim to see if that page or section of the book has the information you want.

• Force your eyes to move very quickly until you find the information you want or decide that it is not there.

To skim a newspaper, magazine, or encyclopedia article, read each subhead and quickly glance at the paragraphs, paying special attention to the first and last sentences of each.

 Exercise 2 | **Practice Skimming to Locate Information**

Force yourself to read at top speed as you look for specific information. Use a daily newspaper to do this exercise.

1. If you watch television tonight at 8 P.M., what program will you choose to watch? What channel is it on? What program is playing tonight on your local public television (PBS) channel at 8 P.M.?

_____

_____

2. What is the main subject of each of the editorials on the editorial page?

_____

_____

3. In one sentence, summarize the most important story in today's newspaper. (A newspaper's most important story is usually in the upper-right-hand column of the front page of the first section.)

_____

_____

4. Write the headline and the name of the author of a story that appears in the sports section. Then summarize the story in one sentence.

_____

_____

Exercise 3 | **Skimming One of Your Sources**

Skim one of the sources you have listed in Step 2, Exercise 14 (page 45), to see if you can find information that is directly related to your topic. Write down the information as it is listed in the source and the page number(s) on which it is located.

1. Title and author of source

_____

_____

2. Information related to (name of topic)

_____

_____

3. Page number(s) where information is located

_____

_____

Interactive Online Tutorial at
www.sadlierresearchpaper.com

Avoiding Plagiarism

In your finished paper, you must not copy the words or ideas of another writer without giving that writer credit. You cannot even come *close* to copying. If you do, you are guilty of **plagiarism**, stealing another person's **words** and/or **ideas** and passing them off as your own. *Plagiarism,* which comes from a Latin word meaning "kidnapper," is totally unacceptable. It is a very serious academic offense and carries very serious consequences.

- Students have received a failing grade on their research papers.
- Students have failed an entire course.
- College students have been expelled and lost their tuition money.
- Authors have lost their reputations and the ability to publish again.
- Publishers have been sued.
- Journalists have lost their jobs.
- Government officials and candidates for public office have resigned.

So don't even *think* about plagiarizing.

INTENTIONAL PLAGIARISM. Teachers are aware that some students copy large chunks of material word-for-word from published or online sources. It's much too easy—dangerously easy—to use the copy-and-paste tools on a word processing program to insert someone else's writing into a paper. Some students may "borrow" an entire research paper (used by someone else in a previous class) and submit it as their own. Some even buy research papers offered for sale on the Internet. This is both unwise and unethical.

Students are always amazed when they are caught, but they shouldn't be surprised. Teachers have a good idea of the writing style and capabilities of each of their students, and they are suspicious whenever phrases, sentences, paragraphs, or sometimes even a whole paper doesn't "sound" like a particular student's work. They can compare the research paper with a student's writing portfolio and get a pretty good idea of whether or not the work is the student's own.

Teachers also can go online to detect cheating. There are plagiarism-detecting tools, such as Turnitin, that allow teachers to scan a student's research paper. Software programs highlight passages that have been taken (word-for-word or very closely) from online sources or other students' essays. Another easy way to detect plagiarism is to use a search engine, such as Google. Teachers can type into a search bar distinctive phrases from a research paper, enclose those phrases in quotation marks, and hit the search button. In an instant, the computer will tell them whether the paper has been plagiarized and, if it has, it will identify the original source.

ACCIDENTAL PLAGIARISM. Accidental plagiarism occurs when you forget that you are quoting a source and don't give proper credit. **Remember:** You need to give credit for someone's *ideas,* not just for someone's *words*. To avoid this kind of plagiarism, it's essential that when you take notes, you distinguish your own words and ideas from those of the author of the source you are using. (For two foolproof techniques, see guidelines 5 and 6 on page 56.) For most writers of research papers, a long time passes between the day they take notes and the day they begin drafting their papers. Therefore, make sure that in your notes, you make it crystal clear who said what.

GIVING CREDIT. A **paraphrase** is a restatement of a writer's ideas in your own words. Suppose you are paraphrasing a writer's ideas from one of your sources. Even though you are not copying the writer's exact words, you are using the writer's ideas. Unless you give credit to the original writer, you are plagiarizing.

It is not enough simply to mention in passing that information you are presenting in your paper is paraphrased from the work of another author. The acknowledgment must be formal: a parenthetical reference to the original source, which is listed on the Works Cited page. (Rules and guidelines for documenting sources are covered in Step 7.) In the example that follows, note that the writer not only refers to the book and the author being paraphrased (*Cosmos* by Carl Sagan) but also cites the page number where the original material is located in that book. (Since the book title is given in the passage, the writer only needs to cite the page.) Had the writer failed to credit the original author in this fashion, he or she would be guilty of plagiarism.

> In <u>Cosmos</u>, based on his thirteen–part ← **title**
> television series, Carl Sagan describes the ← **author**
> extraordinary songs of whales and dolphins.
> Because sight and smell are not much use in cloudy
> ocean waters, Sagan explains, these underwater
> mammals communicate by means of sound. Humpback
> whales have extraordinary memories, and scientists
> have recorded exact repetitions of whale songs
> that last anywhere from 15 minutes to an hour.
> Sometimes groups of whales sing in unison. They are
> clearly communicating, but no one has figured out
> what the songs mean (271). ← **page number in source**

Look carefully at this original paragraph from Leslie Porter's research paper on the Cuban Missile Crisis of 1962. Then look at the note card written by a student who read Porter's paper. The student who wrote the note card is guilty of plagiarism, whether accidental or not.

ORIGINAL TEXT

The Cuban Missile Crisis had acted like a bucket of cold water thrown over the heads of world leaders, who were so frightened by the nuclear danger that they decided that negotiation and communication were of the utmost importance. As a result of the crisis, the following year the United States and the Soviet Union hammered out the Limited Nuclear Test Ban Treaty. Also, a special "hotline" was established for instant communication between the White House and the Kremlin. During the crisis, it had become clear that "seven-hour delays for messages to reach Washington and the reliance on bicycle-riding Western Union messengers were unacceptable means of communication in a nuclear age" (Finklestein 109). These were perhaps the two biggest dividends of the Cuban Missile Crisis.

— Leslie Porter, "The Cuban Missile Crisis"

NOTE CARD

3

Cuban Missile Crisis—bucket of cold water thrown over the heads of world leaders

Frightened by nuclear danger→ need for negotiation and communication

Two biggest dividends of the Cuban Missile Crisis:

1. Hammered out Limited Nuclear Test Ban Treaty—following year
2. Instituted hotline for instant communication between the White House and the Kremlin

pp. 6-7

Which words and phrases are copied word-for-word from the original text? They should be enclosed in quotation marks.

Exercise 4 **Writing a Better Note Card**

On a separate piece of paper or a note card, write a better note card based on the original text from Leslie Porter's paper. Try to express the ideas in your own words. If you use any of Porter's phrases, enclose them in quotation marks.

Here are three examples of plagiarism and one acceptable use of the original text.

Plagiarism Example 1

Kennedy and Khrushchev had a bucket of cold water thrown over their heads by the Cuban Missile Crisis. Frightened by the nuclear danger, they decided it was really important to negotiate and communicate. As a result of the crisis, they hammered out the Limited Nuclear Test Ban Treaty and instituted a special hotline for instant communication between the Kremlin and the White House.

What's wrong: Much of the language is copied word-for-word from the original text. There are no quotation marks, and no source is given.

Plagiarism Example 2

The Cuban Missile Crisis had two good results. The first was that world leaders, after having had a bucket of cold water dumped over their heads, realized that it was really important to negotiate and communicate. They hammered out the Limited Nuclear Test Ban Treaty the following year and "a special hotline was established for instant communication between the White House and the Kremlin." It was unacceptable, they had learned, to have seven-hour delays in communication and to rely on Western Union messengers to deliver messages by bicycle.

What's wrong: The language is much too close to the original text. Although one sentence is enclosed in quotation marks, the source of the quotation isn't identified.

Plagiarism Example 3

After the Cuban Missile Crisis, Soviet and American leaders realized that seven-hour delays for messages to reach Washington and the reliance on bicycle-riding Western Union messengers were unacceptable means of communication in a nuclear age.

What's wrong: Most of this sentence is copied word-for-word from the source quoted in the original text. The writer has not used quotation marks or identified the source.

Acceptable Use of Source

After it was all over, everyone realized that "the Cuban Missile Crisis had acted like a bucket of cold water thrown over the heads of world leaders" (Porter 6). No one doubted the urgent need for instant communication and negotiation between the United States and the Soviet Union. As a result of the great scare of the Cuban Missile Crisis, the Soviet Union, the United States, and Great Britain negotiated the Limited Nuclear Test Ban Treaty in September 1963. The two superpowers (the Soviet Union and the United States) also instituted a direct telephone line—a hotline—between the Kremlin and the White House (Porter 7).

Why this is acceptable: Notice that the direct quote is enclosed in quotation marks, and the source is identified. Other than the quoted sentence, the writer uses her own words but also acknowledges the source of her ideas.

Exercise 5   Identifying Plagiarism

Read the original text below, and then decide whether each of the numbered items at the top of the next page is an example of plagiarism or whether it is acceptable as written. In the space provided, write whether each item is plagiarism (**P**) or acceptable (**A**). Then, rewrite the plagiarized items to make them acceptable.

ORIGINAL TEXT

surfing: sport of gliding toward the shore on a breaking wave. Surfers originally used long, cumbersome wooden boards but now ride lightweight synthetic boards that allow a greater degree of maneuverability. The surfer begins at the point where the waves begin to form, then, facing shore, paddles toward the beach with an oncoming wave. When the wave catches the board, the surfer stands up and glides along the wave's crest—or, in the case of a large wave, in the "tube" formed by its overhead curl. Although the origins of surfing are obscure, it is clear that it developed in Hawaii, where it was popular during the 19th cent. It spread to the California coast during the 1920s and became very popular with American youth in the 1960s. With lifestyles and regimens freer than those of most athletes, surfers comprise a unique sporting subcult. Though surfing is practiced in many other Pacific nations, its mecca remains Hawaii, where the international surfing championships are held annually.

— Excerpt from *The Columbia Encyclopedia*, Paul Lagassé, editor. Copyright © 2007 by Columbia University Press. Reprinted with permission of the publisher.

1. The beginnings of surfing are unknown, but it is clear that it developed in Hawaii, where it was popular during the nineteenth century.

   _____

   _____

2. The center of the surfing world is Hawaii, where each year, surfers from all over the world come to participate in surfing championships (Columbia Encyclopedia).

   _____

   _____

3. "When the wave catches the board, the surfer stands up and glides along the wave's crest."

   _____

   _____

4. Today's surfboards are lightweight and made from synthetic materials, which gives surfers "a greater degree of maneuverability."

   _____

   _____

Taking Notes

When you find information that you think will be useful for your paper, it's time to adjust your reading speed. Slow down from skimming speed to the pace you use when you are trying to understand information. If you are like most readers, that means you will read every sentence, not skipping any words, and concentrate on the meaning of what you are reading. You still will not take notes on everything you find, just on information that you think might be useful for your paper.

☑ **Follow these eight guidelines for taking notes.**

1. Use 3" x 5" cards or 4" x 6" cards (or pieces of paper cut to either of these sizes), or keep notes in a single file on a computer.

2. Write the source number in the upper-right-hand corner of the card. On each card, take notes from only one source.

3. Write on only one side of each card, and write about only one main idea. (You will then be able to arrange and rearrange your note cards easily according to their main ideas.)

4. Write a heading—a key word or phrase—at the top of the note card, and underline it. The heading indicates the main idea discussed on the note card. Usually, the heading is one of the topics or subtopics in your working outline.

5. Make a conscious effort to use your own words when you take notes. It may help to close the book and explain to yourself what the author has written, and then write that explanation on your note card. You do not need to write in complete sentences. Use abbreviations and symbols.

6. Enclose direct quotations in large quotation marks. Make sure you have quoted word for word, *exactly* as the author wrote it. If you wish to leave out any material (a sentence or phrase or even a single word) from the quoted passage, you must show that you have done so by inserting ellipses at the appropriate point. (For more information on ellipses and other changes to quoted material, see Step 6.)

7. At the bottom of each note card, write the page number(s) where you found the information.

8. Before you go on to a new note card, double-check to see that you have written the source number and page numbers. If you haven't done this, your note card will be useless because you will not be able to find and document the source of your information again.

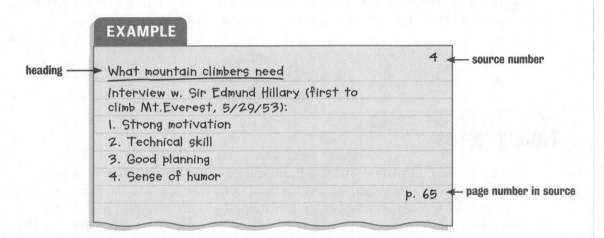

EXAMPLE

heading ——→ What mountain climbers need

4 ←—— source number

Interview w. Sir Edmund Hillary (first to climb Mt.Everest, 5/29/53):
1. Strong motivation
2. Technical skill
3. Good planning
4. Sense of humor

p. 65 ←—— page number in source

e-writing If you have the use of a laptop, you can take it with you to the library (or any other place you visit to find information) and take notes directly on the computer. Or you can keyboard your notes at school or at home. Save your notes in a separate file or document, and be sure to print out a hard copy—just in case something happens to the file or to the computer.

You can make sorting through your notes (the first job in Step 4) a lot easier if you group together all the notes with the same heading (key word or phrase at the top of the note card). Here's how to do it: Write your heading, and then hit the Search or Find command in the Edit menu. Search for that same heading elsewhere in your notes. If you find another note with the same heading, cut and paste it to the same place. Then when you print your notes, you will have them neatly grouped by heading.

Three Kinds of Notes

Your notes will probably contain a mixture of direct quotations, paraphrases, and summaries.

DIRECT QUOTATIONS. Sometimes, you will find a writer's wording so vivid or effective that you decide you might want to quote it in your paper. On your note card, copy the quote exactly, word for word, just as the writer wrote it, and enclose the quoted material in large quotation marks. (Later on, when you review your notes, the jumbo quotes will alert you immediately that the wording isn't yours.)

EXAMPLE

> 1
>
> The Great Gatsby
> F. Scott Fitzgerald letter to Maxwell
> Perkins (editor) about plans for 3rd novel:
> "I want to write something new—something
> extraordinary and beautiful and simple +
> intricately patterned."
>
> p. 112

Hint!

In your finished paper, keep direct quotations brief, and use them sparingly. Think of sprinkling a handful or two of direct quotations throughout your paper. No more than one-sixth of your total paper should be direct quotations.

Exercise 6 — **Taking Notes for a Direct Quotation**

Look through one of your sources until you find a sentence or phrase you might quote directly in your paper. Fill out a note card for that direct quotation.

PARAPHRASES. Remember that when you paraphrase a text, you restate the writer's ideas in your own words. A paraphrase covers every idea in the same order as in the original but is usually shorter. Paraphrases are most useful when you are writing about a short literary text, such as a poem. Here is a paraphrase of Robert Frost's "The Road Not Taken."

> The speaker in the poem remembers a time when he was walking in the autumn woods and came to a place where he had to choose between two roads. He stood there a long time, feeling sad that he could not travel both. After peering down one road as far as he could see, he chose the other, grassier one. Both roads were worn about the same and were covered with fresh leaves. He told himself he would go down the other road someday but didn't really think he would ever be back. He says that he will be telling about this choice many years in the future. His taking the less-traveled road was an important turning point in his life.

As you take notes for your paper, in most cases, you'll be paraphrasing informational prose, not poetry. Here's an example of a factual paragraph and one writer's paraphrase of the ideas in that passage. How well do you think the writer has paraphrased the passage?

ORIGINAL TEXT

Navajo medicine men create sandpaintings, or "dry paintings" as they call them, as part of a ceremony to heal someone who is ill. Sandpaintings are not made to last. They are drawn, used, and destroyed in a single day. To make a sand painting, a medicine man and others who have been trained in the art sit on the earthen floor of a kiva, a large room used for ceremonial purposes. They use dry pigments (such as gypsum, ochre, sandstone, and charcoal) to draw the symbolic figures and designs, beginning with the motif in the center of a large circle. The traditional designs of Navajo sandpaintings have been handed down for hundreds of years, and each design goes with a specific chant. A sandpainting for the Navajo Beauty Chant, for example, depicts various water creatures, while one for the Mountain Chant contains the figures of four bears. When the intricate painting is finished, the person to be healed sits in the center of the painting while the medicine man completes the chant. After the ceremony is finished, the medicine man obliterates the painting.

PARAPHRASE

Sandpaintings, which are part of a Navajo healing ritual, are made to last only a day. Medicine men and others who are specially trained draw symbolic figures and designs, using dry, natural pigments. These traditional designs are unique to each special chant. The sick person sits in the middle of the finished painting while the chant is completed. Afterward, the painting is destroyed.

Exercise 7 **Paraphrasing Information in an Article**

Work with a partner to paraphrase these two paragraphs.

ORIGINAL TEXT

Like light, sound is a form of energy that travels in waves. Sound can travel through air (thunder, voice, animal noises) and through liquids (underwater sounds of whales and dolphins). Sound can even travel through solid matter, as when an earthquake or volcanic explosion causes seismic waves that reverberate through the earth.

Early scientists tried to measure how fast sound travels. An English clergyman and naturalist named William Derham (1657–1735) devised an experiment to measure the speed of sound. In 1708, he climbed to the top of a church in Essex, England. Using a telescope and a pocket watch, Derham timed how long it took for him to hear the sound of a cannon being fired 12 miles away. He could tell when the cannon was fired by seeing the flash of its explosion. Derham's measurements were very close to what we know about the speed of sound today: At a temperature of 68 degrees Fahrenheit (20 degrees Centigrade), sound travels through the air at 1,130 feet per second.

WORKING TOGETHER

Exercise 8 **Paraphrasing a Quotation**

On a separate piece of paper, practice paraphrasing by using your own words to express the ideas in each of the following quotations. When you have finished, get together with a partner or small group to compare your paraphrases. Have you accurately restated the writer's ideas? **Hint:** You might begin your paraphrase by identifying the source. For example, "In a letter that Thomas Jefferson wrote in 1785 to Peter Carr, he said that—"

1. "He who permits himself to tell a lie once, finds it much easier to do a second and third time, till at length it becomes habitual; he tells lies without attending to it, and truths without the world's believing him. This falsehood of the tongue leads to that of the heart, and in time depraves all in its good dispositions."
   — Thomas Jefferson, *Letter to Peter Carr*, 1785

2. "In the new code of laws which I suppose it will be necessary for you to make I desire you would remember the ladies, and be more generous and favorable to them than your ancestors. Do not put such unlimited power into the hands of the husbands. Remember all men would be tyrants if they could. If particular care and attention is not paid to the ladies we are determined to foment a rebellion, and will not hold ourselves by any laws in which we have no voice, or representation."
   — Abigail Adams, *Letter to John Adams*, 1776

Choose an important paragraph from one of your sources. On a separate sheet of paper or your computer, write a paraphrase of it. With a partner, compare your paraphrase with the original text. Have you included all the writer's ideas in the same order as in the original? Have you used *your own* words? Have you credited the original source?

SUMMARIES. When you summarize something, you restate the main ideas in your own words. A summary does not give all the details, only the most important ones. Here, for example, are several paragraphs about utopias, followed by a brief summary:

ORIGINAL TEXT

Do you think you would like to live in a utopia? The word *utopia* is a made-up word that means, literally, "not a place." Sir Thomas More made up the word from the ancient Greek *ou-* (not) and *topos* (a place). More, a prominent English author and statesman, described the island of Utopia in a political essay in 1516. In More's *Utopia*, men and women are equally educated (unheard of at the time), and all religions are tolerated. More's Utopia is an ideal society in which every person thrives, and injustice, poverty, and misery no longer exist. More's *Utopia*, published in Latin, was an immediate success. Unfortunately for More, his conflict with King Henry VIII over Henry's desire to break from the Roman Catholic Church led to More's beheading in 1535.

Gradually, the words *utopia* and *utopian* have come to refer to any ideal society. Since More's day, others have written about such societies, most notably Samuel Butler in *Erewhon* (1872), an anagram of the word *nowhere*, and Edward Bellamy in *Looking Backward* (1888). B. F. Skinner's *Walden Two* (1961) depicts an ideal community based on the writer's behavioral psychology theories. All these utopian works criticize contemporary society and propose remedies for society's ills. Satires of utopian societies abound, including Jonathan Swift's *Gulliver's Travels* (1726), Aldous Huxley's *Brave New World* (1932), and George Orwell's *1984* (1949). The latter two portray *dystopias*, societies in which something is vastly wrong.

SUMMARY

> The word <u>utopia</u> comes from the ideal society Sir Thomas More described in a political essay in 1516. More called his island Utopia, from the Greek for "not a place." Utopian literature does two things: criticizes what is wrong with the writer's society and suggests ways to fix society's injustices and other problems. Other utopian novels include Bellamy's <u>Looking Backward</u>, Butler's <u>Erewhon</u>, and Skinner's <u>Walden Two</u>. Swift's <u>Gulliver's Travels</u>, Huxley's <u>Brave New World</u>, and Orwell's <u>1984</u> are satires of utopias.
>
> 2
>
> p. 426

Keep in mind that when you are taking notes, you do not have to use complete sentences. Words, phrases, and fragments are fine—just as long as you can understand later what you have written on your note card and you make sure to avoid plagiarism.

EXAMPLE

> 2
>
> Meaning of utopia
>
> Utopia (Gr., "not a place"). Made up by Sir Thomas More, name of island & ideal society in his essay <u>Utopia</u> (1516). Utopia & utopian = any ideal society
>
> p. 426

Hint!

If you have printed your source (a newspaper or magazine article, for instance), you can highlight main ideas with a brightly colored, transparent marker. Then when you make your note cards, you can go directly to the highlighted parts of the article.

Exercise 10 — Summarizing Important Information from a Source

Choose one of the sources that you plan to use for your research paper. On note cards or on your computer, summarize each of the important ideas that may be of use to you, using your own words. Be sure to write a heading, the source number (see your bibliography cards), and the number of the page on which you found your information.

Here is a brief passage on the first African American baseball player in the major leagues. On a separate sheet of paper or on your computer, take notes in your own words for a research paper on Jackie Robinson. Compare your notes with those of a partner or small group.

When World War II ended, some people, including reporters, argued that African Americans had fought and died in the war and that it was time to integrate professional baseball. Branch Rickey, the Brooklyn Dodgers' president, agreed. He assigned Dodger scouts to search for a talented player in the Negro Leagues. Rickey chose Jackie Robinson, who was playing shortstop for the Kansas City Monarchs.

According to Rickey's plan, Robinson would play for a year with a Canadian team, the Montreal Royals, the Dodgers' best minor league team. In 1946, he led the league in batting and runs scored, and that year the Royals won the pennant and the Little World Series. The grateful Montreal fans considered him a hero.

On April 10, 1947, Rickey announced that Robinson would become the first African American player in the major leagues. That first season Robinson and his wife received hate mail and death threats. He and his teammates were jeered by fellow baseball players and managers and by fans. And Robinson was turned away from hotels and restaurants that accommodated his teammates. But Robinson never lost his cool, and he played extraordinary baseball that season. Lightning fast, he led the league in stolen bases. His 12 home runs, 175 hits, and great fielding at first base led to his being named Rookie of the Year. Robinson was named the Most Valuable Player in 1949, the year he stole 37 bases and led the league in batting.

When he was inducted into the Baseball Hall of Fame in 1962, Robinson said, "I feel quite inadequate to this honor. It is something that could never have happened without three people. Branch Rickey was as a father to me, my wife, and my mother. They are here making the honor complete." He became the first baseball player—black or white—to have his portrait on a U.S. postage stamp.

Exercise 12 **Practice Taking Notes During an Interview**

Pretend that you have been asked to introduce a classmate at a school assembly. Interview a classmate about his or her earliest memories, family, hobbies, ambitions, and so on. Think of five or six questions, and take notes on your classmate's responses. Introduce your classmate to the class, using the notes you took during your interview.

Exercise 13 **Taking Notes for Your Research Paper**

In each of the possible sources you have discovered, skim until you locate information you think will be useful in your research paper. Then take notes, following the guidelines on pages 55–56. You may end up with dozens of cards from each source. Before you leave each card, double-check to see that you have written the correct source number in the upper-right-hand corner and that you have listed the page numbers where you found the information.

Exercise 14 **Checking Your Progress**

Answer each of the following questions about the work you've done so far.

1. What are the major headings in your working outline? Does your outline follow the form shown on page 48?

   _____

   _____

2. How did you decide when to take notes? How did you locate relevant information?

   _____

   _____

3. What essential information did you put on each of your note cards?

   _____

   _____

4. How have you distinguished direct quotations from your own notes, thoughts, and comments?

   _____

   _____

5. Explain the difference between a summary and a paraphrase. Have you used either of these on your note cards?

   _____

   _____

Checklist Review

Are you on schedule?
Check the Timetables on page 10.

☐ Before you start taking notes, create a working outline.

☐ Skim your sources to locate information for your paper.

☐ Take notes in your own words.

☐ Enclose a direct quotation (the author's exact wording) in large quotation marks.

☐ Follow the guidelines for taking notes on pages 55–56.

☐ Make sure you give proper credit for a writer's words and ideas.

For more on writing a thesis statement and a title, see Step 4 in the two model research papers at **www.sadlierresearchpaper.com.**

Write a Thesis Statement and a Title

CALVIN AND HOBBES © 1993 Watterson. Reprinted with permission of UNIVERSAL PRESS SYNDICATE. All rights reserved.

You have finished—or at least you think you've finished—taking notes. You may have hundreds of notes. What's next? You will be happy to know that the next few tasks are much easier than the ones you have already completed. You are now almost halfway through the job of writing a research paper. Check your progress against the schedule you have set for yourself.

Organizing and Evaluating Your Notes

Before you write a thesis statement and a title for your paper, you will need to pay some attention to your note cards.

☑ Sort your note cards into stacks having the same heading.

Some stacks will be short; some may be quite tall. If you have a great many cards under one heading, perhaps you should divide them into two or three more manageable subheadings. Keep stacks in order by bundling them with rubber bands.

Take time to reread each note card. Make sure that you have got the heading right. You may find cards that might better be classified under different headings.

☑ Evaluate your notes.

If you stopped to read and evaluate information *before* you took notes from your sources, you probably will not have ended up with many unusable note cards. Some students, however, can't resist capturing every scrap of information that might just *possibly* turn out to be useful. Now is the time to get rid of what you are sure you will not use.

BE SELECTIVE. Do you have too much information on one subject? Use only the best—the most interesting, the most pertinent, the most persuasive. But do not destroy or throw away the weaker note cards; you may need them yet. Instead, place them at the bottom of the piles, and mark them in some way (maybe a small red X) so that when you start writing, you will recognize these cards as weaker than the others.

FILL IN THE GAPS. Is there not enough information in some stacks? Go back to the library, find more sources, and take additional notes.

REVISE YOUR OUTLINE. Revise your working outline to fit the information you have found. Consider eliminating any heading or subheading for which you have not been able to find enough information.

ASK, "WHAT'S THIS DOING HERE?" If you have no idea why a note card made it into a particular pile, move it to a more suitable pile, or drop it altogether. You might make a separate pile of possible discards.

Hint! You should end up with a stack of note cards or printouts for each heading and subheading in your working outline. If you don't have at least two notes for each section of the outline, you may not have enough information.

Exercise 1 Evaluating Your Notes

Ask yourself these questions about your notes:

- Can I read what I wrote on each card?
- Does each card have a source number and a page number?
- Is every card directly related to a heading or subheading in my working outline?
- Do I have too little information for some headings?
- Do I have too much information for some headings?
- Does the information on the note card really fit the heading I have put it under? Do I need to move the card to a different heading or maybe discard it entirely?

On a separate sheet of paper or in a new file on your computer, write a brief progress report. Mention any problems you have discovered as you evaluated your notes and what work still needs to be done.

e-writing If you have taken your notes on your computer, you should also have printed out a hard copy to work with. Always back up or keep a hard copy of your work. You can space out your computer notes so that three "note cards" fit on a page. Experiment until you get the spacing right. Then print all of your notes, and cut each page into thirds so that you can sort each note into stacks having the same heading. You may end up with some combination of handwritten note cards and computer-printed notes. No problem. But there is still nothing like handling physical pieces of paper or note cards when you are trying to organize and evaluate your notes.

Unity

☑ **Make sure that all your information fits the scope of your paper.**

Think of the paper's **scope** as a big umbrella that covers all of the paper's main ideas and supporting details. Information that strays outside the paper's scope distracts the reader and destroys the paper's **unity**. As you reread and evaluate your notes, you will develop an even clearer idea of exactly what you are writing about. If you suspect that a note card does not belong under the umbrella, pull it out and set it aside.

For example, if you are writing a research paper on the effects of day care on children under two years old, which of the following studies fit the paper's scope?

1. A study of children under the age of two who spend at least 20 hours a week in day-care centers in Houston, Texas

2. A recent study of the training, qualifications, and experience of day-care workers in New York City

3. A study of the personalities, development, and sleeping habits of 3,000 babies aged two or under who spend more than 10 hours a week in day care

4. A study of the personality differences in one-year-old identical twins in southern California

The first and third studies fit the paper's stated scope. The second and fourth studies do not. Study 2 is about day-care workers, not children in day care. Although study 4 deals with one-year-olds, it does not specify that these children are in day care.

Exercise 2   What Fits and What Doesn't?

Put a check mark in the blank for the items of information that fit the research paper described. Write an X for the items that do not fit and will hurt the paper's unity.

For a research paper on the photographs of the Civil War taken by Mathew B. Brady and his assistants:

_____ 1. Brady's assistants took most Civil War photos; Brady almost blind

_____ 2. History of development of photography

_____ 3. Brady authorized to accompany Union troops and document war

_____ 4. Brady quote about going to Bull Run battlefield: "A spirit in my feet said 'Go' and I went."

_____ 5. Walt Whitman's poems about the Civil War

_____ 6. Brady's portrait photographs of Abraham Lincoln

_____ 7. Causes of the Civil War

Coherence

☑ **Arrange the information in a way that readers will easily understand.**

A paper is **coherent** when it is orderly and makes sense. You have already thought about ordering your ideas (as you wrote your working outline). Now it is time to check and rethink your organization. Arrange and rearrange your stacks of note cards until you are satisfied that the information flows in a logical way.

The three most common ways of ordering information are **chronological** (used to narrate the order of events in time), **spatial** (used to describe a place or object), and **by importance** (used to explain or to persuade). If you use order of importance, you can arrange ideas and details from most to least important or from least to most important. However, you do not have to force one of these types of organization onto your paper. Just concentrate on arranging ideas and details in the clearest, most natural, and most logical way.

Try explaining to a partner or small writing group why you have arranged the sections of your paper as you have, and ask for feedback.

Exercise 3 **Ensuring Coherence**

Check your stacks of note cards against your working outline. Ask yourself the following questions.

- Now that I have sorted and evaluated my note cards, have I discovered any problems in my working outline? If so, how do I propose to fix these problems?

- What feedback have I received from a partner or writing group? What changes, if any, do I plan to make in response to this feedback?

On the lines below, write a brief progress report on any problems you have discovered and changes you plan to make.

_____

_____

_____

_____

  Exercise 4 **What's Wrong with This Working Outline?**

Work with a partner or small group to decide on what's wrong with the following working outline. How would you suggest fixing the outline so that it is coherent and follows the proper outline form? You may find it helpful to review the outline form on page 48.

Chocolate

I. Growing cacao trees

    A. A tropical tree

II. Some great recipes

    1. My mother's recipes

    2. Others

III. Different types of chocolate

IV. Milk and dark chocolate

V. White chocolate

VI. Unsweetened chocolate for baking

VII. History of chocolate

VIII. How chocolate is made

Audience and Purpose

☑ **Identify your audience and your purpose.**

AUDIENCE. The manner in which you express your thesis statement and the way that you focus your paper depend in part on your intended audience. Imagine how a paper on the latest techniques for growing orchids might be tailored for each of the following audiences: members of an orchid club, a group of middle school students, a group of senior citizens who have no gardening experience, and a group of biology teachers.

Audiences vary in what they need to know and want to know. Some of the audiences mentioned would know a lot about growing orchids; some would know nothing. For audiences that know little, you would have to define terms and provide background information. For those who already know a lot about orchids and other plants, you could skip the background and discuss technical details.

Clearly, the primary audience for your research paper is your teacher and your classmates. But can you find a special audience, too? If you are writing about legislation and advertising designed to prevent teenagers from smoking cigarettes, for instance, you might make your paper available to the school's science club or to a local group of advertising professionals.

PURPOSE. If you have not already decided on the purpose of your research paper, now is the time to pin it down. Your purpose will affect which details you choose to include and the way you express your ideas. Are you trying to explain? Are you comparing and contrasting, analyzing causes and effects, or proposing a solution to a problem? Perhaps your purpose is to interpret or evaluate a literary work or works. Whatever your purpose, you will better maintain the focus of your paper if you always keep in mind the way in which you are trying to affect your audience.

Exercise 5   Identifying Your Audience and Purpose

Stop to think about your research paper's audience and purpose. Answer each of the following questions in a complete sentence.

1. Who is the audience for my research paper?

   _____

   _____

2. What does my audience already know about the topic I am writing about? What might they need to know or want to know?

   _____

   _____

3. What other groups of people might be interested in this topic? How can I arrange to share my paper with them?

   _____

   _____

4. What is the purpose of my paper? (If possible, use one of the purposes mentioned on the preceding page, such as "analyze," "interpret," or "explain.")

   _____

   _____

Thesis Statement

☑ **Draft a working thesis statement that tells what you will cover in your paper.**

A thesis statement is a single declarative sentence that states the controlling idea of your research paper. It identifies both your topic and your limited focus and suggests what the body of your paper will cover. Usually, the thesis statement is either the first or the last sentence in the introductory paragraph.

Keep the following guidelines in mind as you draft your thesis statement.

- A thesis statement should not be expressed as a question. If you have phrased your limited topic as a research question, your thesis statement provides a one-sentence answer to that question.

- A thesis statement is a preview of what the paper is about. It states the topic and the writer's specific focus on the topic. (Do not begin with "The purpose of my paper is. . . ." or "In this paper, I will write about. . . .")

- A thesis statement controls the paper's content. Everything in the paper provides support for the thesis statement.

- A thesis statement may suggest—but should not state—your conclusions. Save your conclusions for the end of your paper.

- A thesis statement should have a confident tone. Sound as if you're sure of what you're saying. Avoid using hedge words and phrases such as *probably*, *might*, *I think*, *seems*, *apparently*, and *it seems to me*.

Here are several examples of faulty thesis statements. Note how each has been revised and improved.

EXAMPLE

Wordy and Tentative	**Confident**
It seems to me that probably one of the seriously important decisions almost all teenagers face today is deciding what jobs they might have sometime in the future.	The most important dilemma today's teenagers face is making informed career decisions: choosing a type of work that will sustain them and preparing adequately for that career.
Vague	**Specific**
In this community, crime is a problem that people can work together to overcome.	Crime Watch, a community-based resident patrol, is a practical, effective way for citizens of all ages to cooperate in protecting themselves and their community from crime.
States Topic but Does Not Limit Focus	**States Topic and Limits Focus**
Dogs can be trained to help disabled people.	For thousands of disabled Americans, "service dogs" improve the emotional, social, and economic quality of life.
Question	**Statement**
How can high school students start a school radio station?	With as little as $500, high school students can create and staff a "drive-by" radio station, benefiting both the students and the school in significant ways.

Exercise 6 | **Revising Thesis Statements**

Read each of the faulty thesis statements that follow. Revise each thesis statement so that it meets the requirements stated in the guidelines on pages 70–71. You may make up details if you wish.

1. The purpose of my paper is to write about how strikes in sports have affected fans.

   _____

   _____

2. How do the amount and the kind of television that teenagers watch influence their achievements in school?

   _____

   _____

3. The purpose of my paper is to write about some of the many young-adult novels that deal with important issues that are helpful to their readers, who most likely never see counselors.

   _____

   _____

4. How do weather forecasters make their predictions?

   _____

   _____

5. I really think that something needs to be done about elections in the United States because too few people register to vote and usually only a small percentage of registered voters actually casts ballots in local and state elections and even in the years when there are presidential elections.

   _____

   _____

Exercise 7 | **Drafting a Thesis Statement for Your Paper**

Before you do this exercise, review your working outline and your stacks of note cards. Make sure you have a clear sense of the scope of your paper. Then on a separate sheet of paper or on your computer, write at least three significantly different versions of a thesis statement for your research paper. Choose the thesis statement you like best. Share all your thesis statements with a partner or writing group. Do your own preferences match? Try to explain why the one you have chosen is the best.

Writing a Title

☑ **Draft a working title that reveals your topic and your narrowed focus.**

Your title is the first chance you have to communicate your topic and your focus (the limited part of the topic you're tackling) to your reader. A good title should mention both.

Although you are far from having to finalize your title, a working title and thesis statement will help clarify your thinking and keep you on track as you prepare your final outline (Step 5) and write the first draft of your paper (Step 6).

Keep the following guidelines in mind as you draft your working title.

- A straightforward title is better than one that is cute or too clever. The title should not leave your reader wondering, "What's that about?"

- A colon is helpful. You might write the topic first, followed by a colon, followed by your limited focus. The first word following the colon should be capitalized.

- The title should not be stated as a complete sentence, although it might suggest a question.

Here are some examples of faulty titles. Note how each has been improved.

EXAMPLE

Too Vague Credit Card Problems	**Specific** Using Credit Cards: How to Keep from Going Under
Statement Too Many Children Don't Know What to Do in a Fire	**Revised** Teaching Children What to Do in a Fire
Too General Mystery Novels and Movies	**Specific** Making a Mystery Novel into a Movie: Successes and Failures
Unclear Feeding the Diet Industry	**Clear** The Diet Industry in America: Big Money
Too Cute Escaping with the Wizard of Oz	**Straightforward** Ballooning as a Sport: Advantages and Disadvantages

Exercise 8 Revising Titles

This exercise will give you some practice before you tackle your own title. Clearly, it is difficult to write a good title for a paper you know nothing about, but see what you can do with these titles. Make up whatever you need (usually a focus) to improve the title. Then get together with a small group to compare and discuss your revisions.

EXAMPLE

Playing the Drums

Different Drums Around the World

1. The United Nations

   _____

   _____

2. Creativity Should Be Encouraged

   _____

   _____

3. TV's Greatest Hits

   _____

   _____

4. Special Effects

   _____

   _____

5. Edgar Allan Poe

   _____

   _____

6. Diets for Staying Alive

   _____

   _____

7. Teenagers and Cars

   _____

   _____

8. Popular Music

   _____

   _____

9. Freedom of Speech

_____

_____

10. Buying Online

_____

_____

Exercise 9 **Drafting a Title for Your Research Paper**

On a separate sheet of paper or on your computer, write some titles (at least four) for your paper. Discuss them with a partner or writing group. Choose the one you like best. This can be your working title, and you can change it up until the day you turn your paper in.

Exercise 10 **Checking Your Progress**

Answer each of the following questions about the work you've done so far.

1. What general headings have you used to stack or group your note cards?

_____

_____

2. Do you have too much or too little information in any of your stacks of note cards? What will you do to solve this problem?

_____

_____

3. Which note cards have you discarded? Why?

_____

_____

4. What is your working thesis statement?

_____

_____

5. What is your working title? Why did you choose that title?

_____

_____

Checklist Review

Monday 1 — Are you on schedule? Check the Timetables on page 10.

☐ Sort your note cards into stacks having the same heading.

☐ Evaluate your notes.

- If you have too much information under a heading, discard the notes that contribute the least to your paper.

- If there's not enough information under a heading, find more sources and take notes.

☐ Revise your working outline to fit the information you have found.

☐ Make sure that all your information fits the scope of your paper.

☐ Arrange the information in an order that readers will easily understand.

☐ Identify your audience and your purpose.

☐ Draft a working thesis statement that tells what you will cover in your paper.

☐ Draft a working title that reveals your topic and your narrowed focus.

For more on writing a final outline, see Step 5 in the two model research papers at **www.sadlierresearchpaper.com**.

STEP 5

Write a Final Outline

Reprinted by permission: Tribune Media Services

The last step before you actually start writing your paper is finalizing your outline. If you did a working outline in Step 3, you will need to update and revise it now. But the writing process isn't exactly the same for everyone. You may be a writer who writes first and outlines later. Check with your teacher to see if it's okay to postpone—but not omit—the outline step until after you write your first draft. Keep in mind also that some teachers do not require a formal outline. Ask your teacher whether you will have to submit one.

Content and Organization

Your final outline shows at a glance the two essential aspects of your paper: its content and its organization. Usually, a final outline includes a third element, your thesis statement, which comes right after the title and before the outline of the body of the paper.

The three important parts of a research paper that *never* appear in an outline are the introductory paragraph(s), the paper's conclusion or concluding paragraph(s), and the Works Cited list. You will learn more about these parts of your paper in Step 6 and Step 7.

Hint!

Some teachers do not want the thesis statement to appear in the outline. Find out whether your teacher wants the thesis statement included.

☑ **Choose either a topic outline or a sentence outline.**

Your outline must be either a topic outline or a sentence outline, not a combination of both. You cannot mix the two types of outlines. Your teacher may make the decision for you by specifying which type you will be required to write.

In a topic outline, the headings and subheadings are a series of words or phrases, not complete sentences.

I. Native American "code talkers" during World Wars I and II
    A. Who they were
        1. Their tribes
        2. Their languages
    B. What they did
    C. Why they were so successful
        1. Spoken (not written) languages
        2. Languages totally unfamiliar to enemy code breakers

In a sentence outline, every heading and subheading is a complete sentence. (A complete sentence contains a subject and a verb and expresses a complete thought.)

Each type of outline has its advantages. A topic outline is quicker and easier to write. A sentence outline takes more time but has two distinct points in its favor: (1) It furnishes ready-made topic sentences for your paragraphs. (2) Because it forces you to summarize what you are going to say about each topic, it can reveal problems in the organization of your ideas.

EXAMPLE

I. Native Americans served successfully as "code talkers" in the United States Armed Forces during World Wars I and II.
    A. They were fluent speakers of their native languages.
        1. They were Choctaw, Navajo, Comanche, Winnebago, Kiowa, and Cherokee.
        2. Each tribe spoke a unique language.
    B. Code talkers transmitted military information via walkie-talkie radios and field telephones to other speakers of their language.
    C. Enemy code breakers were unable to understand the American Indians' languages.
        1. Almost all were spoken languages only and had no written form.
        2. These tribal languages were totally unfamiliar to outsiders.

The Form and Logic of an Outline

☑ **Follow the correct outline form.**

The main headings and subheadings are written in a standard form.

- A number or letter precedes each heading. Each number or letter is followed by a period or is enclosed in parentheses.

- The first word in every heading begins with a capital letter. Sentence outlines (but *not* topic outlines) have a period at the end of each heading.

- Indentations show a heading's level of importance. An indented heading is a subdivision of the preceding heading.

Title of Paper

Thesis statement: _____ .

I. Main heading

   A. First-level subheading

     1. Second-level subheading

     2. Second-level subheading

       a. Third-level subheading

       b. Third-level subheading

         (1) Fourth-level subheading

         (2) Fourth-level subheading

           (a) Fifth-level subheading

           (b) Fifth-level subheading

   B. First-level subheading

     etc.

☑ **Identify the major sections of your paper. These will be your main (Roman numeral) headings.**

How can you figure out what the main headings of your outline should be? If you did a working outline to help guide your note-taking (Step 3), you have already made a stab at identifying the main headings and subheadings. Compare your stacks of note cards (separated according to headings) with your working outline. Do you want to change some of the main headings or reword them? Do you want to add new main headings? Do you want to drop some of the main headings?

Hint!

How many main headings should you have? At least three and no more than five. If you do not have enough main headings or if you have too many, rethink the organization of your paper.

When you are figuring out your main headings and subheadings, you are using the critical-thinking skill of **analysis**—that is, you are breaking your topic into its smaller, separate parts. (When you analyze something, you break it into its separate parts and examine each part. For example, you analyze a short story by discussing its plot, characters, point of view, setting, and theme.)

Throughout your outline, make sure that headings and subheadings are **discrete**—that is, entirely separate. Headings and subheadings should not overlap or duplicate each other. There are two things wrong with the main headings in the following example. Can you find them both?

ILLOGICAL

    Topic: Why the movie *The Wizard of Oz* remains an enduring classic

      I. Its plot

     II. Its story line

   III. Its music

   IV. Its visual effects and songs

Main headings I and II are about the same thing (plot and story line mean the same thing), and the "songs" part of heading IV duplicates the "music" of heading III.

LOGICAL

    Topic: Why the movie *The Wizard of Oz* remains an enduring classic

      I. Its plot

     II. Its characters

   III. Its music

   IV. Its special effects

Here are four common types of research papers with examples of how the topic has been broken up into main headings:

1. Examine a problem. Discuss one or more solutions.
    Topic: How to reduce school violence

      I. Statistics past and present

     II. Solution 1: school crime-watch organization

   III. Solution 2: peer mediation program

   IV. Solution 3: increased security

2. Examine an effect. Discuss several causes.
    Topic: What has caused global warming, and how serious is it?

      I. Increased burning of fossil fuels (coal, gas, oil) produces increases in carbon dioxide and other greenhouse gases.

     II. Even small environmental changes may lead to significant global warming.

   III. Clouds may either raise or lower Earth's temperatures.

3. Examine a cause. Discuss several effects.

Topic: Regular exercise and a low-fat diet

   I.   Decrease in heart disease

   II.   Decrease in obesity

   III.   Increase in average life span

4. History of something (a movement, an event, an idea)

Topic: The essay, a relatively new literary form

   I.   First essays (*Essais,* written by French lawyer and scholar Michel de Montaigne, 1533–1592)

   II.   Formal essays (e.g., those written by American essayist, poet, and philosopher Ralph Waldo Emerson, 1803–1882)

   III.   Informal essays (20th century to present)

WORKING TOGETHER   **Exercise 1**   **Analyzing a Topic to Formulate Main Headings**

Use your imagination and common sense to write three or four main headings that might be covered in a research paper on each of the numbered topics that follow. (**Note:** There are no right answers to this exercise, only different approaches to analyzing the topic.) Work with a partner or in a small group, and compare your main headings with those of your classmates.

1. How to increase voter turnout in the United States

   I.   _____

   II.   _____

   III.   _____

   IV.   _____

2. How cell phones have changed American life

   I.   _____

   II.   _____

   III.   _____

   IV.   _____

3. The three (or four) best things about television

   I.   _____

   II.   _____

   III.   _____

   IV.   _____

4. How advertisers persuade you to buy their products

I. _____

II. _____

III. _____

IV. _____

Exercise 2 **Identifying the Main Headings in Your Research Paper**

Write your topic and the working title of your research paper. On the lines below, divide your paper into at least three main headings.

Topic _____

Working Title _____

I. _____

II. _____

III. _____

IV. _____

☑ **Divide the main headings into subheadings and then into sub-subheadings, as needed. You can never have only one subheading; you must have at least two.**

It is not logical to divide a larger heading into only one subheading. (Think of dividing a whole pie into pieces: You can cut the pie many different ways, but unless you have at least two pieces, you have not divided the pie.)

Here is part of an outline showing subheadings and sub-subheadings:

EXAMPLE

```
Topic: Why the movie The Wizard of Oz remains an enduring
       classic
  I. Its plot
     A. Frame of story
        1. Tornado in Kansas
        2. Return to Kansas
     B. Fantastic adventure
     C. Suspenseful conflicts
        1. Good versus evil
        2. Struggle to return home
 II. Its characters
     A. Girl as hero
     B. Sympathetic scarecrow, tin man, lion
```

☑ **Within any level, word the headings so that they are parallel in structure.**

In writing, *parallel* means having the same grammatical structure. In the following example, the headings in A, B, and C are parallel. Each heading is made up of a noun followed by an infinitive phrase (*to* plus a verb).

Hint!

Try this "bottom-up" technique to check the logic of your outline: Read the outline from the bottom up. Each group of lesser subheadings should "add up" to the more important heading above it.

II. Instruments to predict volcanic eruptions

    A. Chemical sensor to analyze gases in volcanic plume

    B. Seismometer (buried sensor) to record vibrations in magma

    C. Sensors to measure cracks in volcano's surface

In the following example, the A, B, and C headings are not parallel.

II. Instruments to predict volcanic eruptions

    A. Chemical sensor for measuring gases in volcanic plume

    B. How a seismometer (buried sensor) is used

    C. Cracks on surface

WORKING TOGETHER | **Exercise 3** | **Parallel Structure**

Revise the headings in the following outlines to make them parallel. (Write your corrections on the page.) Compare your revised headings with a partner's.

```
Topic: Jane Addams and her work

   I. About Jane Addams's life

  II. 1889, helped found Hull House, a settlement house in
      Chicago.

 III. Addams had other interests.

      A. Her work for women's rights

      B. Winning the Nobel Peace Prize
```

```
Topic: Animated cartoons: The technology

    I.  Artists who draw cartoons by hand

        A.  Summary of what makes cartoon characters move

        B.  Earliest short cartoons

        C.  In Walt Disney studios, the famous group of animators
            —the Nine Old Men—who created full-length movies
            such as Bambi, Peter Pan, 101 Dalmatians.

   II.  Animation done by computers

        A.  How it works

        B.  Tron (1984), first computer-animated film

  III.  What is the future of animated cartoons?
```

GUIDELINES

Writing a Final Outline

- Write either a sentence outline or a topic outline. *Don't mix the two types*.
- A number or letter precedes each heading. Each number or letter is followed by a period or enclosed in parentheses.
- Every heading begins with a capital letter. Sentence outlines (but not topic outlines) have a period at the end of each heading.
- Indentations show a heading's level of importance. An indented heading is a subdivision of the preceding heading.
- If any heading calls for subheadings, there must be two or more.
- The wording of headings within a section must be parallel.

WORKING TOGETHER | **Exercise 4** **What Might the Headings Be?**

The note cards in this exercise are for a report on the development of skyscrapers and their effects on the people who live and work in them. The thesis statement for the report is "Two American inventions—steel-frame construction and a safety device for elevators—led to the skyscraper, which altered Earth's human landscape." Read the notes carefully. Then on a separate sheet of paper or on your computer, develop an outline based on them. Try to make your headings and subheadings logical and parallel. Meet with several classmates to talk about your outlines based on these notes.

History of skyscrapers—Chicago   1

Before skyscrapers, masonry (brick or stone) construction—
thick walls at base to support upper stories

Chicago fire Oct.8–10, 1871, destroyed 3 1/2 mi. central city →
building boom

Steel–frame construction (unlike masonry) allowed windows,
more room @ base, greater number of stories

1st skyscraper = 9–story Chicago's Home Insurance Co. Bldg.
1884–85, architect Major Wm. LeBaron Jenney, "father
of the skyscraper" Anecdote: Jenney got steel–frame
construction idea when wife put heavy book on top of metal
birdcage—thin wires supported it

Great Chicago architect—Louis Henry Sullivan.

                                           pp. 539–541

Importance of Elevator   1

Essential invention—elevators

In NYC, Elisha Graves Otis (1811–1861) invented
safety device: stopped elevator from falling if chain
broke; 1st passenger elevator 1857

Otis patented device in 1861, built steam elevators
"vertical railways"—used esp. in hotels; later
powered by electric motors

                                   pp. 537–538

History of word "skyscraper"   2

1794—triangular sail on a clipper ship; original
meaning

1826—high–standing horse

1857—very tall man

1892—person riding a high bicycle

1891—tall building of many stories; first use in
Boston Massachusetts Journal

                                   p. 43

Effects of skyscrapers   3
Residential and business skyscrapers: treat
separately?
Some effects: growth of cities as centers of
commerce, greater population density, less human
scale (no neighbors, no sense of community)
Positive: great views, lots of light, efficient use
of city's limited space
Negative: "too impersonal," hate waiting for
elevators
                                            pp. 430-431

What Lewis Mumford says   3
"If fast transportation made the horizon the limit
for urban sprawl, the new methods of construction
made the 'sky the limit,' as gamblers loved to say."
Acc. to Mumford, urban density "befouled &
poisonous air, constricted housing, demoralized
social life, teeming with violence & crime"
                                            pp. 430-431

What workers say   4
Survey of people who work in skyscrapers
Their fears (safety: dependence on elevators &
electricity; dangerous in earthquake & fire)
Convenient to fast public transportation

Exercise 5 Revising Your Working Outline

Spend some time looking over your note cards and your working outline. As you do
so, ask yourself each of the following questions. (You may want to write down your
answers on a separate sheet of paper or on your computer.) They will help you to
decide what changes you will need to make in your outline.

- Which headings or subheadings need more information?
- Are there headings or subheadings that need to be added?
- Are there headings or subheadings that should be dropped?
- Which headings or subheadings need to be changed or reworded?
- What other changes do I need to make?

Exercise 6 Writing Your Final Outline

On a separate sheet of paper or on your computer, write your final outline.

Exercise 7 Checking Your Progress

Answer each of the following questions about the work you've done so far.

1. What problems did you encounter when you were trying to finalize your outline?

   _____

   _____

2. How did you solve those problems?

   _____

   _____

3. How did you improve your outline as you developed it?

   _____

   _____

4. If you are not on schedule, what do you need to do to catch up?

   _____

   _____

Monday 1 Are you on schedule?
Check the Timetables on page 10.

Checklist Review

- ☐ Choose either a topic outline or a sentence outline.
- ☐ Follow the correct outline form.
- ☐ Identify the major sections of your paper. These will be your main (Roman numeral) headings.
- ☐ Divide the main headings into subheadings and then into sub-subheadings, as needed. You can never have only one subheading; you must have at least two.
- ☐ Within any level, word the headings so that they are parallel in structure.

For more on writing a first draft, see Step 6 in the two model research papers at www.sadlierresearchpaper.com.

Write a First Draft

GREAT MOMENTS in LITERATURE

The first writer's block...

ONCE UPON A TIME,

WILEY

NON SEQUITUR © 1992 by Wiley Miller. Reprinted with permission of UNIVERSAL PRESS SYNDICATE. All rights reserved.

You have passed the halfway mark in the writing of your research paper. You have your note cards and (probably) a final outline. You have drafted a thesis statement and a working title. Now you need to pull it all together in sentences and paragraphs. You will use the critical-thinking skill called *synthesis*. Synthesis is the putting together of all kinds of pieces and parts and creating something new. For a research paper, you start out with lots of raw material— notes about other people's ideas—and you end up with something unique: a paper that is different from anything that anybody has ever written before.

What You Do *Not* Have to Do

Let's start with five things you *don't* have to do when you draft your paper.

1. You absolutely don't have to have a final outline before you start drafting. You may be one of those write-first, outline-later people who asks, "How do I know what I'm going to write until I see what I've written?"

2. You don't have to write the introduction, body, and conclusion in that order. Some people write from the beginning to the end of the paper. Other writers draft the body first and leave the introduction and conclusion until last.

3. You don't have to write the body of your paper in the order shown in your outline. Just start with the main idea that you feel most confident about. Draft that whole Roman numeral section. Then pick another section to attack.

4. You don't have to think about niceties. You need not worry too much about writing perfectly formed sentences at this step. You will have plenty of time for all that later when you revise (Step 8). For the moment, just focus on getting your ideas onto paper or your computer screen.

5. You don't have to panic. If you discover that something is lacking or otherwise amiss, it is not too late to fix it.

Some General Guidelines

Since the writing process is different for everyone, there is no fixed set of rules you must follow as you draft your paper. You may follow the suggestions here, or you may do it your own way. Just make sure that you leave yourself plenty of time to do a good job when it comes time to revise and put your paper in final form.

1. Writing your first draft is a big task, but it is just a beginning. You will make lots of changes (see Step 8) before you are done.

2. Try to write your first draft in one sitting, without interruption. Find a quiet place and stay focused until you have finished. If you cannot finish in one sitting, try to do it in two or three sessions.

3. Follow your outline, but adjust it as needed. If something just doesn't work, drop it. If something needs to be put in, add it.

4. If you are writing an informational, or factual, paper, write in the third person. (Do not mention yourself; do not use the pronouns *I* or *me* or *we*).

5. Find your own voice. Express your ideas as clearly and directly as you can. Do not use fancy-sounding words that you cannot define.

6. Give credit! Do not pass off anyone else's words or ideas as your own. Keep very careful track of your sources, and be sure to document them.

7. Save everything. Do not throw out any of your note cards or (if you have taken notes on a computer) note card documents.

e-writing Be sure to save your work at regular intervals (every 5 minutes or so), even though computers have an autosave function. You do not want to risk losing what you have written if there is a power failure or a computer malfunction. Always keep a second copy of your work (a printout or a backup on a flash drive or a CD).

Using Your Notes

Transforming your notes into sentences and paragraphs is one of the hardest things to do when writing a paper. How do you **synthesize** information from several different sources? Here are some suggestions:

- Check all of your note cards on the specific subject that you're planning to cover in one or two paragraphs.
- Think about what you want to say.
- Write your ideas in your own words unless you are using a direct quotation.
- Express your ideas as clearly and simply as you can.
- Give credit for others' words and ideas. (See Step 7 on parenthetical citations.)

Turning Notes into Paragraphs

In the space below, write five sentences based on information given in the following note cards. Use your own words. Since there are no direct quotes from the source, you cannot use a direct quote in your sentences.

How glass is made   3

Raw materials: sand, sodium carbonate (soda), calcium carbonate (limestone), recycled waste glass
Chemicals added to make colored glass:
red = selenium sulfide; blue = copper oxide
Poured into furnace, heated to 2550 degrees F.
Molded into shapes by machinery, or person (glassblower) blows air through a tube to shape blob of molten glass

DK Science Encyclopedia, p. 110

How glass is made   6

Video of sheets of glass; PPG factory produces 1 million sq. ft. daily for windows
Completely automated except 2 visual inspectors looking for defects in finished glass
Ingredients: mostly sand + soda ash + gypsum + limestone + dolomite + crushed glass
Batches raw materials → melting furnace (melts in minutes) → fining process (bubbles escape) → bath process (liquid glass formed into sheets) → cooled gradually → cut and packed in sheets

PPG Industries, factory in Meadville, PA
www.youtube.com/watch?v=WBA8KrGkQZ4
viewed 9/10/2010

EXAMPLE

The PPG factory in Meadville, Pennsylvania, produces a million square feet of window glass each day.

1. _____

_____

2. _____

_____

3. _____

_____

4. _____

_____

5. _____

_____

 Writing a Paragraph

On a separate piece of paper, use the sentences you wrote in Exercise 1 to write a unified, coherent paragraph about how glass is made. You can change or add to your sentences or get more information from the note cards. When you finish, check your paragraph.

- Have you explained the process clearly?
- Have you used your own words?
- Have you used information from both note cards?

  Writing a Paragraph from Your Note Cards

Take one of your stacks of notes that are on the same topic or have the same heading as your working outline. Choose notes from three different sources, and think about what you want to say about the topic. On a separate sheet of paper or on your computer, write a paragraph based on the information on the note cards. You will be using a critical thinking skill called **synthesizing** as you create a new paragraph from information you've gleaned from three different sources.

When you've finished drafting your paragraph, see if you can improve it. Then get together with a partner to review each other's paragraph and talk about your experience of writing from note cards.

Writing an Introduction

☑ **Write an introduction that attracts your reader's attention and clearly indicates what your paper will be about. Include your thesis statement somewhere in your introduction.**

For a long research paper, your introduction may take one paragraph or several. Often, the thesis statement is the first or last sentence of the introduction. It points the way to the body of your paper, indicating the main ideas you will cover there. Your introduction should also provide background information and define any key terms that readers need to know.

There is no single correct way to introduce your topic. You could probably write five or six distinct and equally effective introductions. In fact, it is a good idea to draft several entirely different approaches and choose the one you like best. Here are some tried-and-true ways that you might consider (but if you come up with something better, by all means use it):

- Tell a brief story (an anecdote).

- Describe a problem or condition.

- Ask a question.

- Cite some startling or interesting fact or statistic.

- Use a powerful or intriguing quote.

Hint!

When you write your introduction: (1) Don't try to be funny. (2) Don't repeat the title. (3) Don't state your purpose: "The purpose of this paper is . . ."

In Step 10, you'll find a model research paper entitled "Lacrosse: Yesterday and Today." The writer begins his paper with a comparison of lacrosse and three familiar sports. He uses these comparisons to capture the reader's attention. The writer's thesis statement is the last sentence in the paragraph.

EXAMPLE

```
    If one goes to a lacrosse game today, one will see a
fast-moving, rough sport that resembles soccer, ice hockey,
and football. Like hockey, lacrosse is a stick-and-ball
game in which players manipulate the ball/puck without
touching it with their hands. As in hockey and soccer,
players try to score points by advancing the ball/puck
past a defending goalie and into the opposing team's
net-shaped goal. As in all three sports, players struggle
fiercely to prevent their opponents from scoring. Like all
three sports, lacrosse is an aggressive game with teams
charging up and down a field. However, as exciting as it
is to watch or play lacrosse today, it cannot compare with
the earliest games of lacrosse played by Native Americans.
```

e-writing If you have written notes on your computer, copy them into the document that you are using for your first draft. You can copy and paste quotations and other ideas where they belong in your draft (in the appropriate paragraph). Then you can reword them or incorporate them into your own sentences. **Be sure to use your own words and to give credit to the original source.**

If you're quoting from a source, double-check to make sure that you've got the quotation exactly right and that you've enclosed the sentence or phrase in quotation marks. If you are using an online source, double-check that the URL is correct.

Exercise 4 Analyzing an Introduction

Read each of the following two introductions to papers comparing two literary works. Then on a separate sheet of paper or on your computer, answer the questions that follow. Meet with a partner or small group to talk about your answers.

> At first glance, it is difficult to see any similarities between Alice's adventures in Wonderland and those of the central character in Hermann Hesse's *Siddhartha*. Alice's adventures are those of a young girl in a world of imagination and nonsense. *Siddhartha* tells of the quest of an Indian boy for spiritual fulfillment. However, when we look at the underlying messages in these books, it becomes clear that what the main characters experience is very similar. Their journeys, so different on the surface, merge into one path. The similarities of Alice's and Siddhartha's adventures can be shown through examination of the characters, their situations, and the novels' symbols.

> What does the white whale represent? What are the various humorous techniques that Mark Twain uses? All the attention focused on questions such as these tends to obscure other important elements of *Moby Dick* and *Roughing It*. These two texts are travelogues; that is, they are records of the places, animals, and people found on journeys into strange and unknown frontiers. The main characters of both books receive an education about the world around them, about other cultures and modes of living; but in doing so, they also receive a thorough education about the values and assumptions of their own societies.

1. From the introductions, can you identify the three main sections (Roman numeral headings) of the research papers? What do you think they are?
2. What, if anything, do you think the writers might do to improve the introductions?

WORKING TOGETHER

Exercise 5 Writing an Introduction

On a separate sheet of paper or on your computer, draft a one- or two-paragraph introduction based on the notes that follow. (The information on the note card is taken from *Solving Your Child's Reading Problems* by Ricki Linksman, who is the director of the National Reading Diagnostics Institute. The book was published in 1998 by MJF Books in New York.) You may make up any details you need. Read your introduction aloud, and then discuss it with a group of classmates.

Kids with Reading Problems   2
Ways to teach young children alphabet & sounds of letters;
4 different types of learning w. suggestions for activities:
1. visual—look for food labels, make collage of newspaper
   letters
2. auditory (hearing)—make up song, sentences w. words that
   begin w. sound
3. tactile (touch)—finger-paint letters; use glue & macaroni,
   sand, sparkles to make letter shapes
4. kinesthetic (motion)—outline letter w. chalk & have kid
   walk the letter

                                                     pp. 130-135

WORKING TOGETHER   **Exercise 6**   Drafting Your Introduction

On a separate piece of paper or on your computer, draft two or three entirely different introductions for your research paper. Share these introductions with a small group of classmates, and ask for feedback. Decide on the introduction you like best.

Writing the Body of Your Paper

☑ **Keep very careful track of your sources. Insert your bibliography source card number after ideas or quotations that need to be acknowledged.**

This is the point where documenting sources can go awry and the possibility of accidental plagiarism occurs. As you review your note cards, watch for those large quotation marks that alert you to a direct quotation. Pay careful attention to ideas that need documenting, too. Plug in parentheses and source card numbers at the appropriate spots. (You will learn all about **parenthetical citations** in Step 7.)

☑ **Write in the present tense. Use the past tense only to refer to historical events.**

This advice about tenses follows the MLA (Modern Language Association) style, which is preferred by most high school teachers. Even though a work of literature was written long ago, it still exists, so the present tense is used to discuss it.

Here are some examples that show the correct use of the present and past tense according to MLA style.

EXAMPLE

PRESENT TENSE	In "I heard a Fly buzz—when I died—," Emily Dickinson **describes** what the speaker in the poem **feels** at the moment of death.
PRESENT TENSE	In his *Philosophiae naturalis principia mathematica* (1687), Sir Isaac Newton **describes** his laws of universal gravity.
PAST TENSE	In 1901, Beatrix Potter **published** *The Tale of Peter Rabbit* privately.
PAST TENSE	Sir Isaac Newton **built** a reflecting telescope in 1668.

☑ **Each paragraph in the body should include a topic sentence that states a main idea. The rest of the sentences should provide supporting details.**

Topic sentences perform two useful functions in informative, or expository, writing—the kind of writing you are doing in a research paper. A **topic sentence** states the paragraph's main idea and also controls the paragraph's content. All the other sentences in the paragraph should support the topic sentence, offering convincing evidence or proof. Try to provide information from at least two different sources to support each topic sentence.

In each of the two paragraphs that follow, the first sentence is the topic sentence. (The parenthetical citations are to the writer's source cards.)

> Sandra Cisneros's prize-winning novel, *The House on Mango Street* (1984), is unusual in that it combines different genres (1). It reads like an autobiography, but it is fiction, which makes it a fictional autobiography. Most critics agree that *The House on Mango Street* is a "Bildungsroman," a German word for a novel about a young person's growing to maturity. The narrator is Esperanza Cordero, who observes her family and friends "in a lyric narrative voice" (2). The novel contains forty-four very short narratives, or literary sketches; some call them vignettes (3). Each of these sketches reads like a miniature short story, and many have been anthologized as separate pieces. Cisneros recalls that her goal in writing *The House on Mango Street* was to write stories that combined poetry and fiction:

I wanted to write a collection which could be read at any random point without having any knowledge of what came before or after. Or that could be read in a series to tell one big story. I wanted stories like poems, compact and lyrical and ending with a reverberation. (1)

Although it is rooted in the Mexican-American community of Chicago, where Cisneros herself grew up, *The House on Mango Street* has a universal theme: the quest for identity. In the novel, the young narrator is "struggling to find a place in her community without relinquishing her sense of self" (3). Esperanza observes the women and girls around her and realizes that "one way to leave house and barrio is to acquire an education" (1). Like Alicia in the vignette "Alicia Who Sees Mice," Esperanza wants something more than to be a wife and mother rolling tortillas. She wants to become a writer.

WORKING TOGETHER

Exercise 7

What's Wrong with This Paragraph?

Get together with a partner to talk about this paragraph from the body of an informational, or factual, research paper.

Many primates have been trained to perform as humans do. I've seen them often, in circuses, in shows, and in movies. You probably have, too. Three out of every five chimpanzees can be trained, while two out of every five orangutans can. Without too much labor and a great deal of difficulty, orangs can sit at a table, eat and drink like humans, ride a tricycle or bicycle, dress themselves, open a lock with a key and even pick the right key out of a half dozen or more, and pound nails with a hammer. One orang learned how to pedal and ride a tricycle in only three lessons—much faster than a small child usually learns.

1. What do you think this research paper is about?

_____

_____

2. What is the topic sentence of this paragraph?

_____

_____

3. Does the paragraph provide enough support for its topic sentence? How many different kinds of support are given?

_____

_____

4. Tell why you do or do not believe the writer's facts and statistics. What is missing from this paragraph?

_____

_____

Exercise **8**   **Writing a Paragraph**

On a separate sheet of paper or on your computer, use the information in the following note cards to write one paragraph for the body of a research paper. (On the note cards, the abbreviation *Q.* stands for Quetzalcoatl.) The title is "The Legends of Quetzalcoatl and King Arthur." The thesis statement is "The ancient Mexican god Quetzalcoatl and the legendary English monarch King Arthur are similar in startling ways."

Legend of Quetzalcoatl   3
Portrayed as plumed (feathered) serpent; the Toltec (pre-
Aztec Mexican people) god who gave corn, learning, arts.
Q. also an actual ruler—sent into exile when high priests
disgraced him, in conflict with sky god.
"Q. the ruler eventually became identified with the god, and
his story is a mixture of history and legend."
Legend of his promise to return important to Aztecs, 16th c.:
Exiled from Tula; made a raft of serpents & set off across
sea; vowed to return to reclaim his throne in year called "I
Reed."
(My note: Something like King Arthur's leaving on a boat,
vowing to return when Britain is in need. Is Q. like King
Arthur? Compare & contrast them?)
                                                        pp. 19-20, 25

note card

source card

                                                        3

Warburton, Lois. Aztec Civilization. San Diego, CA: Lucent
        Books, 1995. World History Ser. Print.

Legend of Quetzalcoatl   5
Q.'s rivalry with Tezcatlipoca, war god. Q. = "Father and
Creator, the source of agriculture, science, and the arts.
He was an enlightened god, the morning star and the evening
star."
Various versions of Q.'s death: sailed toward east on raft
of serpents; parted Gulf of Mexico's waters & walked away;
became morning star; smoke from funeral pyre; ➔ quetzal
birds. All have in common: prophecy that one day he would
return.

                                            pp. 75–76
[My note: see also 2-page mural of Q.'s life, pp.62–63 by
Mexican artist Diego Rivera.]

                                                          3

Josephy, Alvin M., Jr. 500 Nations. New York: Knopf, 1994.
    Print.

Legend of King Arthur   6
Legendary Celtic warrior-king, 5th–6th c., who fought
Saxons
Reigned at Camelot w. knights of Round Table (A. & his
knights represented "ideal of medieval knighthood and
chivalry")
A. killed in battle, body borne away by boat to isle of Avalon;
prophecy of his return someday

                                                          6

The Columbia Encyclopedia. 6th ed. New York:
    Columbia UP, 2001. Web.

 Exercise 9 **Writing the Body of Your Research Paper**

On separate sheets of paper or on your computer, draft the body of your
research paper.

Writing the Conclusion

Here is a common mistake: You are so glad to be finished with the body of your paper that you lose momentum and concentration, and your paper ends with a thud. Avoid this mistake by spending just as much time working on your conclusion as you did on the introduction.

☑ **Write a conclusion that brings your paper to a satisfying close and says something worthwhile.**

Instead of just rephrasing your thesis statement, see if you can leave the reader with something to think about. Try these approaches:

- Offer a judgment.
- Make a final comment or observation.
- End with a quotation that pulls it all together.
- Summarize your main idea(s).
- Refer to your introduction.

In this concluding paragraph, the writer mentions several examples of media coverage at the time of the Cuban Missile Crisis and ends with a final comment, or judgment, about the events and their aftermath.

> At the time of the Cuban Missile Crisis (October 1962), observers recognized that the crisis held tremendous significance for the United States and for the whole world. "The ships of the U.S. Navy were steering a course that would be marked boldly on the charts of history," *Life* magazine proclaimed. "The steel perimeter clamped around Cuba by the U.S. could be the trip-wire for World War III" (1). *Newsweek* predicted that the crisis "may turn out to have consequences of incalculable importance for this century" (2). Things could have turned out very differently than they did, but the prudence and caution of both President Kennedy and Soviet premier Nikita Khrushchev turned this crisis into an opportunity for peace.

Here is a writer's conclusion for a research paper about the life and works of the American poet Theodore Roethke. Read the conclusion and then answer the questions that follow.

> Theodore Roethke was a bold and brilliant poet whose explorations of nature and his own soul gave us some of the best and most unusual poetry in American literary history. His poetry was greatly influenced by his early years and is perhaps all the more searing because it cost him so much inside—cost him, at times, his very sanity. However, as Robert Boyers says:
>
> > It is his triumph that his best poems permit us to embrace the principle of change as the root of stability; that his best poems, through rhythm and syntax and diction, so evoke passion that we are able actively to sympathize with his sense of loss; and that we can feel, with him, how all finite things reveal infinitude. (5)
>
> In all these things, Roethke is truly unique. Theodore Roethke's poetry shows us the pattern of the universe by showing us the pattern on a leaf; he gives us a glimpse of himself, and in doing so gives us an unforgettable glimpse of ourselves and all mankind.

1. Based on this conclusion, identify the two main sections (Roman numeral headings) of the research paper.

   _____

   _____

2. Do you think this conclusion would be better or worse without the long quotation from Robert Boyers? Explain why you think so.

   _____

   _____

3. What, if anything, do you think the writer could do to improve this conclusion?

   _____

   _____

Exercise 11 Writing a Conclusion for Your Research Paper

On a separate sheet of paper or on your computer, write at least two different conclusions. Read them aloud to several classmates, and ask for their feedback. Then decide on the one you think is best.

Using Direct Quotations

Some of your note cards probably contain direct quotations that you think you might use in your paper. As you were taking notes, you enclosed them in large quotation marks just to make sure you would know they are not your own words, and you also checked them carefully for accuracy.

☑ **Follow the conventions for using direct quotations. Make sure that you clearly identify the source of the quotation.**

In the examples that follow, the numbers in parentheses indicate the bibliographical source card numbers of the quotes (and in poetry, the line numbers also). These are temporary citations only. You will learn about **parenthetical citation** in Step 7.

Hint!

Do not use too many quotations (an overload gets boring), and keep them fairly brief. Also, do not keep quoting from a single source. Use a sprinkling of direct quotations from different sources.

PROSE QUOTATIONS

- Run prose quotations into the text if they are four typed lines or shorter.

At the beginning of a sentence

"You gain strength, courage and confidence by every experience in which you really stop to look fear in the face," Eleanor Roosevelt writes (14).

At the end of a sentence

Eleanor Roosevelt, who was painfully shy as a young woman, might have been writing about herself when she declared, "You gain strength, courage and confidence by every experience in which you really stop to look fear in the face" (14).

Interrupted quotation

"You gain strength, courage and confidence," Eleanor Roosevelt writes, "by every experience in which you really stop to look fear in the face" (14).

- You do not have to quote whole sentences. Enclose words or phrases in quotation marks, and run them into your own sentences.

Ernesto Gallarza describes both the difficulties and kindnesses he experienced in the course of "the Americanization of Mexican me" (12).

- If a prose quotation is longer than four typed lines, set it off from the rest of the text. Start a new line and indent ten spaces from the left margin. Do not use quotation marks for these long quotes.

    Jane Austen sets the tone and theme of her comic novel *Pride and Prejudice* in its opening sentences:

        It is a truth universally acknowledged, that a
        single man in possession of a good fortune must
        be in want of a wife. However little known the
        feelings or views of such a man may be on his first
        entering a neighborhood, this truth is so well
        fixed in the minds of the surrounding families,
        that he is considered as the rightful property
        of some one or other of their daughters. (2)

QUOTATIONS FROM POEMS

- Run in three or fewer lines quoted from a poem and use a slash mark (/) to indicate the end of a line. Enclose the quoted lines in quotation marks. (The line numbers of the poem are shown in parentheses.)

    Walt Whitman's "Song of Myself" begins with these
    lines: "I celebrate myself, and sing myself,/ And
    what I assume you shall assume,/ For every atom
    belonging to me as good belongs to you" (1.1—3).

- When quoting more than three lines from a poem, write each line as it appears in the poem. Indent the quoted lines, and do not use quotation marks.

    In "The Raven," his most famous poem, Edgar Allan Poe
    bombards the reader with a whole gamut of sound
    effects to produce a chilling, hypnotic effect:
        Once upon a midnight dreary, while
            I pondered, weak and weary,
        Over many a quaint and curious
            volume of forgotten lore,
        While I nodded, nearly napping,
            suddenly there came a tapping,
        As of someone gently rapping,
            rapping at my chamber door.
        "'Tis some visitor," I muttered,
            "tapping at my chamber door;
                Only this and nothing more." (1—6)

ELLIPSES AND BRACKETS

- Use an ellipsis (a series of three periods separated by spaces) to show where you have omitted words in a quotation. If the quotation comes at the end of a sentence, add a fourth period as end punctuation.

  In his introduction to *A Tale of Two Cities*, Shuckburgh compares Madame Defarge to Lady Macbeth, calling the Defarges "among the greatest—and most terrible—of Dickens's creations, perhaps of all...fiction."

  Charles Dickens begins *A Tale of Two Cities* with a description of the year 1775: "It was the best of times, it was the worst of times...."

- Use brackets to enclose words that you insert in a quotation in order to make the meaning clear.

  U.S. Senator William Fulbright told the Senate, "We are handicapped by [foreign] policies based on old myths rather than current realities" (12).

Exercise 12 — Using Direct Quotations

Write sentences that incorporate all or part of each quotation. Punctuate each quotation correctly. Write your sentences on a separate sheet of paper.

EXAMPLE

"We know the human brain is a device to keep the ears from grating on one another."
  —Peter De Vries, *Comfort Me with Apples* (1956), ch. 1

In Comfort Me with Apples (1956), American novelist Peter De Vries observes, "We know the human brain is a device to keep the ears from grating on one another."

1. "I have a dream that one day this nation will rise up and live out the true meaning of its creed: 'We hold these truths to be self-evident: that all men are created equal.' "
   —Dr. Martin Luther King, Jr., August 28, 1963, at the March on Washington, DC

2. Polonius, Laertes's father, saying farewell to his son:
   This above all: to thine own self be true,
   And it must follow, as the night the day,
   Thou canst not then be false to any man.
   —Act I, scene 3, lines 78–80, *Hamlet* by William Shakespeare

3. "There are only two or three human stories, and they go on repeating them-selves as fiercely as if they had never happened before."

　　—Willa Cather (American novelist), in *O Pioneers!* Chapter 4, Part II (1913)

4. Two stanzas from "The Tiger":

　　When the stars threw down their spears,
　　And water'd heaven with their tears,
　　Did He smile His work to see?
　　Did He who made the lamb make thee?

　　Tiger, tiger, burning bright
　　In the forests of the night,
　　What immortal hand or eye
　　Dare frame thy fearful symmetry?

　　　—William Blake (1757–1827) in *Songs of Innocence and Experience*

5. An excerpt from a speech by Chief Joseph of the Nez Percé tribe to his people after he surrendered to General Nelson A. Miles, October 5, 1877:

　　"Hear me, my chiefs. I am tired. My heart is sick and sad. From where the sun now stands, I will fight no more forever."

Using Indirect Quotations

You can also refer to someone else's ideas by using an **indirect quotation**, which usually begins with the word *that*. Indirect quotations reword the writer's ideas and don't require quotation marks, but you still must identify the source.

Exercise 13 **Using Indirect Quotations**

Hint!

If you can't reword a phrase, enclose a few words in quotation marks.

On a separate sheet of paper or on your computer, write an indirect quotation for each numbered item.

EXAMPLE
"No man is above the law and no man is below it; nor do we ask any man's permission when we require him to obey it."
　　—Theodore Roosevelt, *Third Annual Message*, December 1903

In his Third Annual Message, President Theodore Roosevelt said that nobody is "above the law" or "below it," meaning that everyone must obey the law.

1. "I am not an Athenian or a Greek, but a citizen of the world."
　　　—Socrates, from *Plutarch, Of Banishment*

2. "Facts are stubborn things; and whatever may be our wishes, our inclinations, or the dictates of our passions, they cannot alter the state of facts and evidence."

   —John Adams, from his argument in defense of the British soldiers in the Boston Massacre trials, December 1770

3. "OATS—A grain which in England is generally given to horses, but in Scotland supports the people."

   —Samuel Johnson, Definition of *oats* from his *Dictionary*, 1755

4. "Everything that grows
   Holds in perfection but a little moment."

   —William Shakespeare, *Sonnet 15*

5. "If a man does not keep pace with his companions, perhaps it is because he hears a different drummer. Let him step to the music which he hears, however measured or far away."

   —Henry David Thoreau, *Walden*

Using Graphics

☑ **Think about how you might use graphics to present information.**

Research papers used to be made up of only text, but now teachers may require that you include at least one graphic element in your paper. Learn how to insert charts, photographs, and other **graphics** on the word processing program that you are using.

CHARTS OR TABLES. A graphic made up of columns and rows is called either a chart or a table. Charts and tables let you present a great deal of factual information in a small amount of space. You may copy a chart from a source or create your own chart from information you have gathered. Use the Table menu on your word processing toolbar to create your chart. Charts and tables have a table number above the chart. On the line below the table number, write a title for your chart. Then identify the source in smaller type below the table.

Hint!

For step-by-step instructions on inserting graphics into a Word document, search the Internet using key words such as *insert, graphic,* and *Word document.*

Table 1. Number of High School Lacrosse Players in the United States

Year	Boys	Girls	Total
2007	119,826	81,424	201,250
2006	101,667	67,958	169,625

Source: *US Lacrosse* Member Participation Survey 2007.

DIAGRAMS OR GRAPHS. You're familiar with many kinds of diagrams (pie chart, horizontal graph, bar graph) from your math and social studies classes. Sometimes, a pie chart is just what you need to summarize factual information involving numbers. Or you might use a bar graph like the one to the right to report results of a survey you have taken. Unlike tables, all other graphics are labeled as figures. Place the figure number and title immediately below the figure. On a separate line and in smaller type, give full information on your source.

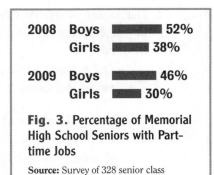

Fig. 3. Percentage of Memorial High School Seniors with Part-time Jobs

Source: Survey of 328 senior class members, Jan. 2008 and Feb. 2009.

PHOTOGRAPHS. A picture, the saying goes, is worth a thousand words. You may use an original photograph (such as a family photo or a photo you have taken), or you may copy an image or photograph you find online. Here, for example, is a photograph of part of a letter Abraham Lincoln wrote to General Joseph Hooker. A writer whose research paper focuses on events in the year 1863 during the Civil War could reproduce a letter from the era.

Source: Library of Congress, Rare Book and Special Collections Division, Alfred Whital Stern Collection of Lincolniana.

Consult your word processing program for directions on how to insert a photo into your text. To copy an image you find online, highlight the image, then right-click on it (if using a PC) and go down to "copy" to paste the image into your paper. Be sure to identify the photograph with a figure number and title, and give full credit to the source.

MAPS AND DRAWINGS. You'll need to give to a map or drawing a figure number and title and also to give full credit to the source.

SPREADSHEETS OR DATABASES. You'll need special software (like Excel) to create a spreadsheet or database. This type of graphic is most useful for original research that involves numbers or statistics. Perhaps you've surveyed your entire class on a current issue and want to present your results in easy-to-read numbers. Ask your school's media specialist or a computer science teacher (or a friend or relative who knows how to do it) for help in creating your spreadsheet. Also, find out how to insert the spreadsheet into your research paper.

Exercise 14 Using Graphics in Your Research Paper

On a separate piece of paper or on your computer, brainstorm why and how to use graphics in your research paper. What kind of graphic(s) might you use to present information you already have? Where will you place each graphic in your paper? Why might it be better to use a graphic in some cases than to present your information in words? Do you have all the information you need to give the source of each graphic?

Exercise 15 Checking Your Progress

Answer each of the following questions about the work you've done so far.

1. What did you attempt to do in your introduction? How might you improve the introduction?

_____

_____

2. How many pages did you write? Do you feel that the body of your paper is about the right length? Too short? Too long?

_____

_____

3. Did you follow your final outline? (Did you work from an outline?) Do you need to revise your outline?

_____

_____

4. Did you use all of your note cards? Which ones did you not use, and why?

_____

_____

5. Did you write a topic sentence for every paragraph? Do you have adequate support for each topic sentence?

_____

_____

6. How pleased are you with the draft of the body of your paper? What work still needs to be done?

_____

_____

7. Did you include quotations in your draft? Were they direct quotations or indirect quotations?

_____

_____

8. Can you identify any points that could be supported by adding a table or chart to your draft?

_____

_____

9. What did you attempt to do in your conclusion? How might you improve the conclusion?

_____

_____

10. What do you need to do next?

_____

_____

Checklist Review

Monday **1** Are you on schedule?
Check the Timetables on page 10.

☐ Write an introduction that attracts your reader's attention and clearly indicates what your paper will be about. Include your thesis statement somewhere in your introduction.

☐ Keep very careful track of your sources. Insert your bibliography card number after ideas or quotations that need to be acknowledged.

☐ Write in the present tense. Use the past tense only to refer to historical events.

☐ Make sure each paragraph in the body includes a topic sentence that states a main idea. The rest of the sentences should provide supporting details.

☐ Write a conclusion that brings your paper to a satisfying close and says something worthwhile.

☐ Follow the conventions for using direct and indirect quotations. Make sure that you clearly identify the source of each quotation.

☐ Think about how you might use graphics to present information.

For more on documenting sources, see Step 7 in the two model research papers at www.sadlierresearchpaper.com.

Document Sources

PEANUTS reprinted by permission of United Features Syndicate, Inc.

In Step 6, you completed the first draft of your research paper. Let it sit for a time while you do two tasks (parenthetical citations and your Works Cited list) that are important but less taxing than writing. In fact, this step, documenting your sources, is probably the easiest one of all. Check your progress against the timetable you have selected. Are you on schedule?

Parenthetical, or In-Text, Citations

When you wrote your first draft, you carefully put your bibliography source card number in parentheses whenever you needed to give credit for a quote or an idea. This form of documentation was only temporary. Now it is time to do it the right way.

☑ Follow the style of documentation that your teacher specifies.

Most teachers prefer the MLA style of parenthetical documentation, which is the style followed in this book. (See Appendix C for a discussion of APA style.) A parenthetical citation is a shorthand reference to the Works Cited list at the end of your paper. It gives minimal information about a source (author's last name, page number on which the information was found), just enough for readers to locate the source in your Works Cited list.

Whenever you insert a parenthetical citation, you have two things to decide:

- where to place the citation
- what information belongs inside the parentheses

☑ Give credit for every quotation and paraphrase.

You will want to document accurately any words or ideas that you have borrowed, but it is not necessary to document common knowledge or every single sentence. Try not to overload your paper with citations.

Hint!

You must document your sources in *both* of these ways: (1) parenthetical citations within the text, and (2) a Works Cited list at the end of your paper.

WHERE TO PLACE A PARENTHETICAL CITATION. Here are some rules governing the placement and punctuation of citations.

> **Place a citation at a natural pause—that is, at the end of a sentence or after a phrase or clause.**

"A turkey, for example, was worth a hundred seeds. A small rabbit was worth thirty" (Burleigh 10).

According to the *MLA Handbook,* the end of a sentence is preferred. However, a parenthetical citation should always come near the quotation or paraphrase it documents. Consequently, it may fall in the middle of a sentence.

They were something like today's coaches (Vennum 28) except that they had—or claimed to have—magical powers.

> **Place a citation at the end of a text sentence and before the end punctuation mark.**

Unripe pods are green, but they change to yellow or purple-red when they ripen (Burleigh 5).

> **If a citation follows a quotation at the end of a sentence, place the citation after the final quotation marks and before the sentence's end punctuation.**

Twenty-two-year-old Thomas Jefferson praised chocolate as "superior to coffee or tea for health and nourishment" (Beach 3).

> **A citation in the middle of a sentence comes before a comma, a colon, or a semicolon.**

"A full-scale blockade generally has been interpreted as an act of war," the *Miami Herald* reported ("Blockade"), and everyone feared what might happen.

> **For a long quote set off from the rest of the text, place the citation on the last line of the quote following the end punctuation mark. Follow this style for both prose and poetry.**

Oren Lyons, honorary chairman of the Iroquois National Lacrosse team, remembers:

> But I should mention that in 1890 the Iroquois were sanctioned against playing at all. Before that we were always part of the international games. We taught the English how to play, we taught the French how to play, we taught the Canadians and the Americans. We were quite active in the late 1800s. We had three trips to England, played in front of Queen Victoria, and they couldn't beat us so they called us professionals and wouldn't allow us to play anymore. (Dellinger)

WHAT INFORMATION GOES INSIDE THE PARENTHESES. The form of the citation varies depending on the source. Use the following guidelines. **Remember:** Every parenthetical citation functions as a quick reference to the full entry on your Works Cited page.

One author

Enclose in parentheses the author's last name and the page number where the quotation or idea can be found. Do not use any punctuation between the name and page number. Write the page number only. Do not use the word *page* or *pages* or the abbreviation *p.* or *pp.*

Canadians who settled in the northeastern states founded lacrosse clubs in Baltimore, Boston, and Philadelphia (Fisher 57).

If the author's name appears in the text, write only the page number in parentheses.

According to Hoyt-Goldsmith, players wore animal charms, such as a hawk feather or bear claw, so that the animal's spirit would help them during a game (13).

If you refer to a complete work, omit page numbers.

In 1990, the government released a whole series of documents directly related to the Cuban Missile Crisis (*National Security Archive*).

More than one work by an author

Follow the styles shown in these examples:

Our first glimpse of the "metallic" Miss Murdstone makes us fear for the young David (Dickens, *David Copperfield* 46; ch. 4).

"It is a far, far better thing that I do, than I have ever done," says Sydney Carton at the end of *A Tale of Two Cities* (Dickens 380; ch. 15).

Two or more authors

If there are two authors, cite both authors' last names. Do not include the word *edited* or the abbreviation *ed.* in the citation.

Gradually, they darken from tan or white or light pink to dark brown, and then they are packed in bags and sold (McFadden and France 32–33).

If there are three or more authors, either cite every author's last name or use the first author's name followed by *et al.* ("and others"). Use the same style (authors' names or *et al.*) in your Works Cited list.

In philosopher Karl Popper's "open society," everyone is free to criticize government without fear of punishment. It is the opposite of a totalitarian society (Bullock, Stallybrass, and Trombley 608).

In 1993, infectious diseases killed 16.5 million people worldwide, more than three times the number who died from cancer (Brown et al. 115).

No author

If no author is given, use the title or a shortened version of it (as given in the Works Cited list). Use quotation marks for the title of an article or editorial. Italicize the title of a book.

Carolus Linnaeus, a Swedish botanist, classified more than 4,400 species of animals and 7,700 species of plants ("Linnaeus").

Electronic sources

For an article accessed from an online subscription service (via a library), cite the author's last name or a title if no author is identified.

Canadians popularized lacrosse and took it over (Taylor).

Cite the writer of an e-mail message. If the Works Cited list has two works by the same person, specify the e-mail message.

Fearing nuclear attack, people descended on supermarkets for canned foods, water, candles, and batteries (Grunwald).

For a page on a Web site, cite the name of the Web site. You won't need a page number since there are no page numbers on a Web site.

What kinds of careers will be most in demand in the next ten years, and what do you have to do to prepare for these jobs? This information is compiled by the U.S. Departments of Labor and Education and can be found online ("Career Voyages").

Hint!

There is no set rule about when to include the author's name in a text sentence and when to refer to it only in the parenthetical citation. Either way is acceptable. Write what seems most natural to you. Your goal is simply to identify clearly the source of the quotation or paraphrase.

For an electronic book (e-book), cite the author's last name and the page number. (Unlike Web sites, e-books do have page numbers.)

In the first century A.D., a Chinese astronomer named Chang Heng devised the earliest known tool to measure movements deep inside the earth. This early device, a *seismometer*, consisted of a pendulum connected to a wheel having eight spokes, each of which had a dragon's head with a bronze ball in its mouth (Lerner 517).

For an image (photograph, work of art, map) found online, cite the artist's name and title of the work. If the artist is unknown (as for a map), cite the title.

One of the Metropolitan Museum of Art's Impressionist paintings shows a young mother focusing intently on her sewing while a child (probably a girl of 4 or 5) leans into her lap (Mary Cassatt, "Young Mother Sewing").

For a video, cite the title of the video.

On April 4, 1968, Robert Kennedy spoke movingly to a mostly African American audience in Indianapolis, Indiana. Kennedy, a presidential candidate, informed his audience of the assassination of Dr. Martin Luther King, Jr., and asked them to respond to the news with love, wisdom, compassion, and a commitment to justice ("Robert F. Kennedy").

Mentioning the Source Within the Sentence

You can avoid parenthetical citations by identifying the source within your sentence. (Later, you must refer to that source in your Works Cited list.)

Note how in the following examples, information about the source is included as part of the sentence.

- In a Web site called "Career Voyages," the U.S. Departments of Labor and Education provide information about the salary, training, and future prospects of people in dozens of careers.
- In act V, scene 5 of Shakespeare's tragedy, Macbeth calls life "a tale/ Told by an idiot, full of sound and fury,/ Signifying nothing."
- In his Internet article "The Irony Hangs Thick at a Game of Lacrosse," Drew Hayden Taylor states that Canadians popularized lacrosse and took it over.

Compare the third example above with the first example under "Electronic sources" on page 112. Note how the same source information can be presented either within a sentence or by using parentheses.

Part of a work with many volumes

Cite the volume number followed by a colon and the page number(s). Don't write the words *volume* or *page*.

In *Contemporary Literary Criticism*, many critics, among them American poets Stanley Kunitz and W. D. Snodgrass, comment on and analyze Roethke's poetry (8:455, 459).

To cite an entire volume in a parenthetical citation, write the author's name, a comma, the abbreviation *vol.*, and the volume number.

> *The Gathering Storm* is an authoritative account of the beginnings of World War II (Churchill, vol. 1).

Two or more works in a single citation

Separate the citations with a semicolon.

> Thirty years later, reporters interviewed people who had played crucial roles in the crisis, among them Curtis LeMay and John Scali (Rhodes; Hernandez).

Quotation from an indirect source

If you are quoting from an indirect source, write the abbreviation *qtd. in* before the source. Whenever possible, however, try to quote from the original source. Sometimes, as in the following example, the original source is not available, and you have to credit an indirect source.

> "Better to have met the issue squarely in Cuba," an editorial in the *Boston Herald* proclaimed, "than later in Berlin or Turkey or even Paris" (qtd. in "Excerpts").

Literary work

For prose works that appear in many different editions, cite the chapter (ch.), part (pt.), or section (sec.) number.

> Uriah Heep threatens his employer, Mr. Wickfield, with what he knows: "Let sleeping dogs lie—who wants to rouse 'em? I don't. Can't you see I am as umble [humble] as I can be?" (*David Copperfield*, ch. 39).

Cite the act and scene numbers of plays: (*Ham.* 2.1) or (*Ham.* II.i).

> On hearing that his wife is dead, Macbeth laments:
>> Life's but a walking shadow, a poor player
>> That struts and frets his hour upon the
>>> stage,
>> And then is heard no more; it
>>> is a tale
>> Told by an idiot, full of sound
>>> and fury,
>> Signifying nothing. (*Mac.* 5.5)

Cite the line numbers of poems: ("Hope" 1–4).

> Roethke recalls his student Jane, who died when she was thrown from a horse, "And how, once startled into talk, the light syllables leaped for her,/ And she balanced in the delight of her thought" ("Elegy for Jane" 3–4).

Hint!

If you need to insert a citation that is not covered by any of these style rules, refer to the *MLA Handbook for Writers of Research Papers*, 7th edition.

Exercise 1 — What's Wrong with These Citations?

Fix them. Pay careful attention to placement, content, and punctuation. Write the sentence, with the citation, on a separate sheet of paper or on your computer. (**Hint:** You will not need all the information given.)

1. Also, Alice and Siddhartha both went through an initiation, an increased awareness of the world. For Alice, it was when she realized that the Queen and her court were "nothing but a pack of cards" (this quote is in Chapter 12 of *Alice's Adventures in Wonderland*, which appears in many different editions), not authority figures to be respected and obeyed without question.

2. Anne Woods, the British television producer, is famous for having developed and produced an international hit TV series for preschoolers, *Teletubbies*. Now she has another show in the works, *Boohbah*. This is an exercise show aimed at preschool children. (I got this information from an article in the *New York Times Magazine*, January 4, 2004, pages 18+. The article is titled "She Speaks 3-Year-Old," and it was written by Susan Dominus.)

3. In "The Greek and Roman Writers of Mythology" (found on pages 21–23 in the preface to her classic *Mythology*), Edith Hamilton mentions some of the sources she uses for her lively retellings of ancient Greek myths (*Mythology* by Edith Hamilton in the Mentor paperback of the Little, Brown hardback edition, copyright 1940 and 1942 by Edith Hamilton.)

4. A beautiful and exciting book of photographs and text called *Eagle* is intended, its author Terrence N. Ingram says, to give readers a close look at the lives of these magnificent birds. In his Introduction, Ingram states: "With their power, beauty, and strength, eagles have been considered a symbol of greatness by many different cultures throughout history." (*Eagle* by Terence N. Ingram was published by MetroBooks in New York. The quotation from the Introduction appears on page 12.)

WORKING TOGETHER

Exercise 2 — Be a Peer Editor

Give this writer a hand by correcting all mistakes in parenthetical citations. Follow the MLA style of parenthetical documentation. This is a good exercise to do with a partner or small group if your teacher approves. (**Hint:** When a poem's title is mentioned in the text, cite only line numbers.)

```
    The poetry of Theodore Roethke (1908–1963) has other

literary influences. Stanley Kunitz notes "throwbacks"

to nursery rhymes, folk literature, counting songs, the
```

Bible, and Blake. "But," he adds, "the poems, original and incomparable, belong to the poet and not his sources." (Stanley Kunitz, pages 102 and 103. A further influence is the poetry of both T. S. Eliot and W. B. Yeats. In Roethke's *Words for the Wind*, for instance, the poem "The Dying Man" is "in a voice almost indistinguishable from Yeats's" (W. D. Snodgrass, pp. 104–105). Some critics have attacked Roethke's imitation of Yeats, calling it a sign of weakness on Roethke's part and a lack of his own ideas and insight (Ralph J. Mills, Jr., page 30).

Roethke's poems are intensely personal. He takes the evolution of self as a theme in much of his poetry, occasionally relating it to another, or a beloved. (Pages 30 and 31 in Mills). An example of the self theme is found in the poem "Open House":

> My secrets cry aloud.
>
> I have no need for tongue.
>
> My heart keeps open house,
>
> My doors are widely swung.
>
> An epic of the eyes
>
> My love, with no disguise.

(These are lines 1–6 from the poem "Open House." I found this poem on page 718 in *The New Oxford Book of American Verse*, edited by Richard Ellmann, © 1976, Oxford University Press.)

Exercise 3 **Writing Parenthetical Citations**

In the space provided, write a parenthetical citation for the work or works given. Read each numbered item carefully before you write the citation. Much more information is provided than you will need. Provide only the information required, and be sure to enclose the citation in parentheses.

1. A reference to a brief feature called "You Be the Judge" by José Schorr. The article appears on page 82 of the *Saturday Evening Post* in the March/April 2004 issue.

   _____

2. An article entitled "Eskimo" on page 927 of *The Columbia Encyclopedia*, 6th edition, 2000. No author is listed.

   _____

3. "China's Behavior in Tibet," a letter to the editor of the *New York Times,* written by Vembar K. Ranganathan. The letter appeared on March 14, 2009, on p. A16.

   _____

4. A paraphrase of an idea in an article by Nicholas Confessore. The article is entitled "What Makes a College Good?" It appeared in *Atlantic Monthly* magazine on pages 118+ in the November 2003 issue of the magazine.

   _____

5. *Women's Rights in the United States: A Documentary History*. The editors are Winston E. Langley and Vivian C. Fox. The citation refers to a chart near the beginning of the book, entitled "Significant Dates in the History of Women's Rights," which appears on pages xxxi–xxxiii.

   _____

6. A reference to the entire book *The Diversity of Life* by Edward O. Wilson. *The Diversity of Life* was published in 1999 by W. W. Norton & Company.

   _____

7. A quotation from *500 Nations: An Illustrated History of North American Indians* by Alvin M. Josephy, Jr., published in New York by Alfred A. Knopf in 1994. The reference is to material entitled "A Clash in the Arctic," pp. 173–181. Josephy's name appears in the sentence that ends with the citation.

   _____

8. A quotation (lines 14–17) from a poem by Theodore Roethke entitled "Elegy for Jane." The research paper cites six other poems by Roethke.

   _____

9. Reference to the entry for "Underground Railroad" on pages 1915–1918 of *Africana: The Encyclopedia of the African and African American Experience,*

edited by Kwame Anthony Appiah and Henry Louis Gates, Jr. The book was published in New York by Basic Civitas Books. It was copyrighted © 1999 by Kwame Anthony Appiah and Henry Louis Gates, Jr.

10. A four-line quotation from the beginning of Canto I (on page 3) of *The Inferno of Dante* by Dante Alighieri, in a new verse translation by the American poet Robert Pinsky. The book was published in New York in 1994 by Farrar, Straus and Giroux.

Exercise 4 **Writing Parenthetical Citations for Your Paper**

Change each temporary citation in your draft to its proper form. When you write your citations in your draft, check the placement, content, and punctuation of each citation.

Works Cited List or Bibliography

☑ **Prepare your Works Cited list, an alphabetical list of all the sources you have referred to in your paper. Place the Works Cited list at the end of your research paper.**

The entries in this section follow the MLA style for documenting sources, which is the style most often required by high school and college teachers. Be sure to follow exactly the style of documentation your teacher requires.

Arrange entries in the Works Cited list alphabetically, and follow the style shown on page 119.

The style for entries in the Works Cited list is exactly the same as the style you used for bibliography source cards in Step 2 (see pages 37–42). You do not have to memorize the style; you just have to know where to find it so that you can refer to it when you have a question about style.

Hint!

What if you're missing information about one or more of your sources? Page numbers? Year of copyright? City of publisher? You'll have to go back online or return to the library (or wherever you located your source) and find the missing information. If you were very careful preparing your bibliography source cards, you won't be missing anything.

To prepare your Works Cited list, all you have to do is to put your bibliography source card entries in alphabetical order and write them on a separate sheet of paper at the end of your research paper. The Works Cited list should contain entries for *every source you actually use* in your paper, *not* every source you consulted. Your bibliography card list will probably be much longer than your final Works Cited list.

Instead of a Works Cited list, your teacher may require a **bibliography**, which lists *all the sources you consulted* while doing your research. A bibliography follows exactly the same format and style as a Works Cited list. Use the Works Cited list below as a model for proper form.

Works Cited

"About Lacrosse." *US Lacrosse*. 3 Mar. 2009. Web. 7 May 2009. <http://www.lacrosse.org/the_sport/index.phtml>.

Dellinger, Laura M. "Asserting Sovereignty Through Sports; Iroquois Lacrosse Teams Compete Internationally Using Tribal Passports." *The Native Voice* 25 Jul. 2003, sec. D: 4. *ProQuest*. Miami-Dade Public Lib. Web. 28 Feb. 2009. <http://mdpls.org/>.

Fisher, Donald M. *Lacrosse: A History of the Game*. Baltimore: Johns Hopkins UP, 2002. Print.

Hoyt-Goldsmith, Diane. *Lacrosse: The National Game of the Iroquois*. New York: Holiday House, 1998. Print.

"Lacrosse." *The Columbia Encyclopedia*. 6th ed. 2001. Print.

"Lacrosse." *Encyclopedia Americana*. 2001 ed. Print.

Mirra, Gerald B. "American Indian Lacrosse." *Whispering Wind* 31 Oct. 1998: 20. *ProQuest*. Miami-Dade Public Lib. Web. 27 Feb. 2009. <http://mdpls.org/>.

Nicholson, Lois. *The Composite Guide to Lacrosse*. Philadelphia: Chelsea House, 1999. Print.

Tanton, Bill. Message to the author. 16 Feb. 2009. E-mail.

Taylor, Drew Hayden. "The Irony Hangs Thick at a Game of Lacrosse." *Wind Speaker* Jun. 2002: 5. *General Reference Center Gold*. Miami-Dade Public Lib. Web. 28 Feb. 2009. <http://mdpls.org/>.

Vennum, Thomas, Jr. *American Indian Lacrosse: Little Brother of War*. Washington, DC: Smithsonian Institution Press, 1994. Print.

"Women's Lacrosse." *The Book of Rules*. New York: Checkmark Books, 1998. Print.

WORKING TOGETHER

Exercise 5 | **What's Wrong with Each of the Following Works Cited Entries?**

Work with a partner to fix each of the following Works Cited entries. Refer to the style for writing entries on pages 37–42. Write your corrected entries on a **separate** sheet of paper. Then compare your changes with those of other students.

1. Kotlowitz, Alex, "All Boarded Up" from the *New York Times Magazine*. March 8, 2009. Pages 28–35 and 42 and 47.

2. Rockwell, Anne. *Open the Door to Liberty: A Biography of Toussaint L'Ouverture.* © 2009, published by Houghton Mifflin in Boston.

3. *Harriet Tubman: The Road to Freedom*, a biography by Catherine Clinton. Boston: Little, Brown. © 2004

4. Donald L. Barlett and James B. Steele. "Why We Pay So Much for Drugs" in *Time*, 2 February 2004. Pages 45–52.

5. *The World Wildlife Fund Book of Orchids* by Jack Kramer © 1989, NY: Abbeville Press

6. E-mail sent from Allan Q. Zambie to the author. This e-mail was sent and received on January 30th, 2010.

WORKING TOGETHER

Exercise 6 | **Writing Your Works Cited List**

On a separate sheet of paper or on your computer, write a draft of your Works Cited list. Include all of the sources you have actually mentioned in your first draft. Alphabetize the sources, and list them in the proper form. Exchange papers with a partner, and check each other's lists for proper style (content and punctuation).

Exercise 7 | **Checking Your Progress**

Answer each of the following questions about the work you've done so far.

1. Have you double-checked to make sure that every quotation and paraphrase has a parenthetical citation?

_____

_____

2. How did you decide when to give a citation and when *not* to?

_____

_____

3. Are you absolutely sure that each parenthetical citation provides the appropriate information and is correctly punctuated?

_____

_____

4. How many works have you listed in your Works Cited list? Is each work credited within your paper?

_____

_____

5. Have you included in your Works Cited list the number and types of sources your teacher specified in the assignment?

_____

_____

Checklist Review

Monday 1 **Are you on schedule?**
Check the Timetables on page 10.

☐ Follow the style of documentation that your teacher specifies.

☐ Give credit for every quotation and paraphrase.

☐ Prepare your Works Cited list. Place the Works Cited list at the end of your research paper.

For more on revising, see Step 8 in the two model research papers at **www.sadlierresearchpaper.com.**

Revise the Draft

BALDO ©2007 Baldo Partnership. Reprinted with permission of UNIVERSAL PRESS SYNDICATE. All rights reserved.

It is now time to revise your first draft. If you have kept to your schedule, you should have plenty of time to do the job properly. It is important that you not rush through this critical phase of the writing process. Revising is the step that will transform a tentative, rambling first draft into a focused, coherent research paper. When you revise, you must look carefully and critically at what you have written.

Before You Start

Revising certainly does not mean just one quick rereading. You need several readings (a minimum of four or five), with time to think about problems you discover and time to come up with solutions. If you have followed the general guidelines in the timetable on page 10, you will have at least two full days for revising. Use all the time available to you. There is a lot left to do.

DO IT YOURSELF. You need to do most of the hard work of revising—evaluating your paper's weaknesses and strengths and deciding what to drop, add, and change— yourself. The approach to revising suggested in this step will help you to focus on each aspect of your paper.

PEER EDITORS. You can benefit from the feedback of peer editors at any point in the revising process. Usually, however, your first draft is so rough that it's not helpful to share it with anyone. Wait until you have revised your draft thoroughly at least once, and then exchange papers with one or more of your classmates. Read each other's papers carefully. Most of all, you want to know whether your readers understand what you are saying and whether they are confused or puzzled by any parts of your paper.

e-writing Do your revising on a hard copy of your first draft. Use a colored pen so your changes will be easier to see. Double- or triple-space your draft to give yourself plenty of room to write in your changes. Copy your first draft into a new document. Then type in the changes you have made on the hard copy. That way, you won't lose anything in your earlier draft. Consider using your word processor's Track Changes function to record your revisions.

☑ **Read your paper several times, focusing on a different aspect each time.**
Revising is a complex task, and it is impossible to look for everything all at once. Force yourself to stay focused on one aspect of your paper at a time. Read through once for unity, a second time for coherence. Start from the beginning, and focus on each paragraph, checking for topic sentences and adequate support. Later, you will focus on each sentence and, still later, on word choices. In Step 9, you will proofread your paper. But if you spot a mistake in spelling, punctuation, or grammar as you are revising, fix it now.

When you are revising, use the common proofreading symbols to indicate changes. Even though you are probably familiar with these symbols (∧ indicates an insert; ¶ means the beginning of a new paragraph), you will find them listed on page 139 of this book.

The Paper as a Whole

☑ **Check to see that you have met all of your teacher's requirements.**
Check the length of your paper, the number of sources, the parenthetical citations, the Works Cited list, and the manuscript form (see Step 10). Unless you have met all the requirements of the assignment, you are asking for trouble. If you think your paper is running a page or two shorter or longer than the required length, talk with your teacher to see if it will still be acceptable.

Hint!
If your paper is running long, cut back wordiness rather than support. If it is running short, go back to your notes to see if you can find additional, relevant material that you haven't used.

☑ **Focus on the paper's unity.**
The paper as a whole and individual paragraphs are said to have **unity** when everything works to develop the main idea of the paper.

DOES EVERY MAIN IDEA IN THE BODY OF THE PAPER RELATE DIRECTLY TO THE PAPER'S THESIS STATEMENT? Your outline should help you here because you dealt with this problem when you constructed it. Check what you have written against your final outline. If any paragraphs have wandered away from the umbrella of the thesis statement, either rewrite the paragraphs to bring them back under that umbrella or delete them entirely. Stay focused on your thesis statement.

DOES EVERY SENTENCE IN A PARAGRAPH SUPPORT ITS TOPIC SENTENCE? When you are drafting, your thoughts may stray off course a little. It is time to delete anything that does not speak to a paragraph's main idea. (Check now, also, to see that each paragraph provides adequate support for the topic sentence.)

ARE YOU SURE IT IS ONLY ONE PARAGRAPH? Sometimes a long paragraph seems strangely unfocused because it really should be broken into two separate paragraphs. Remember to begin a new paragraph whenever you start writing about a whole new idea, and make sure that each paragraph has a topic sentence. Note how the passage that follows has been revised to achieve unity.

EXAMPLE

The American poet Theodore Roethke was greatly influenced by his childhood spent in the Michigan countryside, especially the time he passed in his family's greenhouse, observing nature. ~~Roethke, in case you haven't ever heard of him, was an American poet. He won many awards, and he died in 1963.~~ As a young boy Roethke spent a great deal of time working with his father and uncle in the greenhouse, and this seemed to impress itself on his mind. In later years, he tended to view himself and the world through green-colored glasses, seeing everything as related to and intertwined with nature. (Flowers, plants, earth, and greenhouse images appear in many of his poems.) One example of this greenhouse influence appears in the poem "The Minimal": "I study the lives on a leaf/ the little sleepers, numb nudgers in cold dimensions/ Beetles in caves, newts, stone-deaf fishes." ~~I really like the images in "The Minimal."~~ ¶A second important influence in Roethke's life was the sudden death of his father in 1923 when Roethke was 15. His father's death seemed to tear apart Roethke's sense of peace and security. Roethke's deep hurt shows in much of his poetry. Critic Robert Boyers points out one example of the father's influence on Roethke's later work:

In the poem "Otto," named for his father, Roethke
recaptures the sense of pride he felt in a parent
who controlled a rural environment immersed in
the sounds and stinks and inconsistencies of
nature.(209)

Exercise 1 — What's Wrong with This Paragraph?

Revise the following passage, focusing on questions involving unity. Write your
changes directly on the text. **Hint:** Consider breaking the passage into two or more
paragraphs.

Few people realize that the snake is not always a
creature to be feared. Aside from sea snakes (all of
which are water cobras and highly venomous), only about
one-tenth of the world's snake species are poisonous. In
the United States, according to the *Merck Manual*, the
fraction drops to about one-sixth (about 20 poisonous
snakes out of 120 species). In the United States, more
than 45,000 people are bitten by snakes each year, but
fewer than 1 out of 5 are poisonous bites, and only about
15 people die from snake bites each year (*Merck* 2565).
In fact, many snakes do a great deal of good. "Snakes are
of major importance as pest controllers because of their
extensive predation on destructive mammals such as rats
and mice" (*Columbia* 2546). They also kill wild pigs, small
game in the jungle, and many harmful insects. In many
localities, especially in India, the cobra, which is a
highly poisonous snake, is held sacred and therefore leads
an almost semidomesticated life. More than 20,000 deaths
in India each year are attributed to the bite of poisonous
snakes. According to Hegner, the fact that a pair of

cobras has come to live under the floor of the village temple is a good omen rather than an evil one (125). In fact, if a cobra decides to settle down in your house, it is considered a sign of prosperity. In Europe, white storks are also considered good luck, and people build platforms on their roofs so storks will build their nests there (*Columbia* 2628). A dish of water or milk is put near the cobras' lair each day, and no one disturbs them, for they help to kill the rats, which are a real pest in most Indian villages. "Of course," Hegner reports, "accidents *do* happen, and some people who step carelessly are bitten and die" (126). My cousin Jerrod stepped on a black snake once, but nothing happened to him.

Exercise 2 Revising for Unity

In one sitting, revise your first draft, focusing only on unity. You may want to read through your whole draft once and then carefully reread each paragraph.

Coherence

A paper has **coherence** when the ideas are clearly and logically presented and the writer's thoughts are easy to follow.

☑ Focus on the paper's coherence.

Check to see that ideas are presented in a logical order. You have already thought about the order of ideas as you planned your outline, but the actual writing sometimes reveals an order that seems more logical. (Any order is logical if it makes sense to the reader.) If you are writing about a topic that has a history, you will probably present your information chronologically, moving from past to present and maybe on to the future. Or you might present your ideas in the order of importance, or moving from general to specific, or in a problem-solution or cause-effect sequence.

Hint!

If your revisions involve reordering paragraphs or sentences, try reading them aloud to see how the new order sounds. You can use the cut-and-paste commands on a computer to see how your rearranged paragraphs read.

USE DEVICES TO HELP ENSURE COHERENCE: PARALLEL STRUCTURE, REPETITION OF KEY WORDS, CLEAR PRONOUN REFERENCES, TRANSITIONAL EXPRESSIONS. You know these devices from the writing you have been doing throughout your school career. They are important because they help readers follow your thinking.

Parallel structure

The poems "Bright Star" by John Keats and ~~Robert Frost's~~ "Choose Something Like a Star" *by Robert Frost* both discuss certain qualities in a star that may be desirable in *a person.* ~~human beings.~~

Repetition of key words

Keats is much more flowery and tends to use softer, more flowing ~~words~~ *language*, as when he talks about a "soft fall and swell" on the "new soft-fallen waste of snow." Frost, however, is much more down-to-earth and ~~is more~~ *uses* simple *r* and *more* direct *language.* When ~~the~~ *Frost's* star says, "I burn," the speaker's response is, "Talk Fahrenheit, talk Centigrade." ~~The~~ *Frost's* speaker asks the star to "use language we can comprehend," and that is exactly what ~~the poet~~ *Frost* does.

Clear pronoun references

~~The poet~~ *Frost* alludes to ~~his~~ *Keats's* star in his poem, but ~~his~~ *Frost's* vision of a star is distinctly his own, and in the end, ~~both~~ *the two* poets reach separate conclusions.

Transitional expressions

On the other hand, Frost, instead of just choosing a quality in a star that he likes, is waiting for some sort of message. *At first,* The star will only say, "I burn," but *in the end, it* tells us that we should not only be steadfast but *(like Keats's star)* have a certain loftiness as well.

Here is a list of some useful transitional words and phrases grouped according to the logical relationships they suggest.

SHOWING IMPORTANCE: above all, first (second, third, etc.), last, mainly, more important, most important, to begin with

SHOWING TIME ORDER: after, at first, at last, at the same time, before, during, eventually, finally, first (second, third, etc.), in the end, later, meanwhile, next, once, soon, then, when, whenever, while

SHOWING CAUSE AND EFFECT: as a result, because, consequently, for, in effect, in the end, since, so, so that, thus, therefore

SHOWING COMPARISON: also, and, another, besides, both, in like manner, like, moreover, not only—but also, similarly, still, too

SHOWING CONTRAST: although, but, despite, however, in contrast, in spite of, nor, nevertheless, on the other hand, on the contrary, still, yet

SHOWING AN EXPLANATION: for example, for instance, in fact, in other words, specifically, that is, thus, to illustrate

WORKING TOGETHER

Exercise 3   **Revising for Coherence**

Revise each passage below so that the writer's ideas are clearly and logically presented and the writer's thoughts are easy to follow. Write your revised sentences on the lines provided or on a separate piece of paper. **Hint:** There is no single correct way to revise these passages. You may combine sentences, reorder ideas, or make any other changes to improve the passage's coherence.

1. Light is essential to the process green plants do to make sugars and starches. It is called photosynthesis. Light is solar energy. Solar energy is energy from the sun's rays.

_____

_____

2. One more essential element in it is water. Carbon dioxide is another essential thing for it to happen. And don't forget that light is necessary for photosynthesis to take place.

_____

_____

3. Chloroplasts contain chlorophyll. It is a green pigment necessary for photosynthesis. In most plants, the process of photosynthesis takes place in the leaf. It specifically takes place in special structures called chloroplasts within the leaf.

_____

_____

4. Green plants manufacture food and oxygen. Green plants use raw materials found all over the earth. The raw materials are light, water, and carbon dioxide. Plants provide two things essential for humans and animals to survive on Earth.

Exercise 4 — Writing a Unified, Coherent Paragraph

Write a unified, coherent paragraph based on information in Exercise 3. If you wish, you may use some of your revised sentences from Exercise 3. Write—and revise— your paragraph on a separate sheet of paper. Compare your finished paragraph with those written by classmates. Remember that these devices help to ensure coherence:

- parallel structure
- clear pronoun references

- repetition of key words
- transitional expressions

Exercise 5 — Revising for Coherence

Revise the following passage, writing your changes directly on the text. Compare your corrections with those of your classmates. Does everyone agree on what the problems are? Have you suggested different revisions?

> Everyone dreams, and only a small percentage of those dreams are remembered. There are many theories about what causes dreams. Some psychologists think that dreams are a window into the subconscious, an important sign of inner thoughts and buried feelings. Sigmund Freud believed that dreams represent wish fulfillments. Some insist that dreams are a forgetting process, a way to get rid of unwanted or annoying emotions. Others propose that dreams are a mechanism that enables the brain to get rid of unwanted impulses and memories. Complex networks of cells in the cerebral cortex form faulty connections. During waking hours, these connections give rise to fantasies, obsessions, and hallucinations. When people are asleep, the cortex is cut off from its normal input and output. The lower brain sends random impulses. These cause dreams.

Exercise 6 — Revising for Coherence

Read your whole paper once through for coherence. Then focus on each paragraph, and see if you can make your ideas easier to follow and understand. Insert transitional words and phrases wherever you think they will help clarify ideas.

Sentences

☑ **Focus on each sentence and on the way that related sentences work together.**

VARY SENTENCE BEGINNINGS. The normal order of English sentences is subject + verb + complement(s), if there are any. (Direct objects, indirect objects, predicate adjectives, and predicate nominatives are all called **complements** because they complete the meaning of a sentence.) This word order is built into your thinking; it is probably the way you talk. But if every sentence in your paper begins with the subject followed by the verb, your writing quickly becomes monotonous. Here are some ways to vary sentence beginnings:

Hint!

Try reading your whole paper aloud to yourself, to a partner, or to your writing group. Sometimes you can *hear* problems—awkward or monotonous sentences—that aren't obvious when you're reading silently.

- Begin with a **single-word modifier** (an adjective or adverb).

    Certainly, Henry David Thoreau's experiment at Walden Pond would have to be called a success.

- Begin with a **transitional expression**.

    Of course, one of the reasons Thoreau went to Walden Pond was to experience its extraordinary beauty.

- Begin with a **phrase**.

    At the pond, Thoreau says, he learned that as life is simplified, "the laws of the universe will appear less complex...." Stripping his life to the bare essentials, Thoreau looked inward and outward and found what he was sure was the truth. *To understand Thoreau's experiment*, we must first understand the transcendentalist philosophy of Ralph Waldo Emerson.

- Begin with a **subordinate clause**.

    When he returned to nature, Thoreau found life beautiful and full of possibilities.

VARY SENTENCE LENGTH AND STRUCTURE. In an average paragraph some sentences will be short (especially those with the ideas you want to emphasize); others will be long. You don't have to count words or tally types of sentences, but it is important to create variety within your paragraphs. Remember that sentences can be classified into four types, according to their structure. (In the following examples, main clauses are underlined once, and subordinate clauses are underlined twice.)

- A **simple sentence** has one main clause and no subordinate clause.

  Volcanologists are searching for a safe way to predict eruptions.

- A **compound sentence** has two or more main clauses and no subordinate clause.

  One new device analyzes gases from the plume of smoke above the volcano's crater, and it can be used from a safe distance.

- A **complex sentence** has one main clause and at least one subordinate clause.

  The inventor is a scientist who survived a sudden, violent eruption of a volcano in the Colombian Andes.

- A **compound-complex sentence** has two or more main clauses and at least one subordinate clause.

  Dr. Stanley Williams, who was taking measurements in the crater at the time of the eruption, survived, but six of his fellow volcanologists died when the volcano erupted.

COMBINE A SERIES OF SHORT, CHOPPY SENTENCES.

CHOPPY: English police officers are called bobbies. They are named after Sir Robert (Bobbie for short) Peel. Peel founded the London Metropolitan Police. Irish police officers are called peelers. They are also named after Sir Robert Peel.

COMBINED: English police officers are called bobbies and are named after Sir Robert Peel, who founded the London Metropolitan Police. Irish police officers, also named after Peel, are called peelers.

Exercise 7 Revising Sentences

Read and revise the following passage directly on the text. Vary the sentence beginnings. Combine some sentences to vary sentence length and structure. Feel free to reword, rearrange, and generally improve this paragraph. You may want to cut whole sentences, delete words, and change words. Get together with three or four of your classmates to share your revisions and talk about your changes.

There have been some great contributors to psychology. One of these people was B. F. Skinner. B. F. Skinner was an American psychologist. He lived from 1904 to 1990. Skinner was a behavioral psychologist. Skinner believed that psychologists should study human behavior. They should not focus on concepts that cannot be observed. Behavior can be shaped or learned. Skinner believed this. Behavior can be shaped with positive reinforcement. Positive reinforcement includes praise and rewards. It can also be shaped with negative reinforcement. Punishment and yelling are examples of negative reinforcement (Green and Sanford 186–87).

AVOID WORDINESS AND UNNECESSARY REPETITION. Don't fall into the trap of expressing your ideas in a wordy, convoluted way. Say everything clearly and directly.

Migrating birds face ~~all kinds and sorts of~~ **many** obstacles. ~~when they are migrating.~~ For instance, ~~one of the obstacles is~~ a lighthouse, ~~which~~ may confuse birds, ~~and they'll often run right into the lighthouses,~~ **which are** attracted by ~~the lighthouse's~~ **its** light. When the Washington Monument was first built, ~~in Washington, D.C., it caused the death of~~ hundreds of small ~~flying~~ birds, ~~who lost their lives~~ **died** when they crashed right into **it.** ~~the Washington Monument.~~ Migrating birds have **also** ~~unfortunately ceased to live when they have~~ crashed into newly constructed bridges and ~~brand new~~ buildings. ~~that didn't used to be there.~~

Use all your knowledge about revising to improve the following paragraph. Work especially on the way the sentences hang together. Write your revisions directly on this paragraph. When you have finished, copy your revised paragraph on a separate sheet of paper or your computer. Compare your revised paragraph with those of your classmates. **Remember:** The paragraph should support your thesis statement.

The book *A Connecticut Yankee in King Arthur's Court*, by the writer Mark Twain, tells the story of a man from Hartford, a city in Connecticut, which is why the book's title refers to "a Connecticut Yankee." The man is named Hank Morgan. Morgan is struck on the head by a crowbar. A man named Hercules hits him with a crowbar. The two are fighting. After this happens, Morgan wakes up to find himself in the sixth century. Morgan was the foreman of an arms factory that manufactured weapons in 19th century Hartford, Connecticut. Morgan sets out to bring the civilization of the 19th century into King Arthur's Court in the sixth century. Morgan comes into conflict with an old man whose name is Merlin. Merlin is the court magician in King Arthur's Court. He also comes into conflict with the ignorance and superstition of the ordinary people who live in sixth-century England. Mark Twain's novel *A Connecticut Yankee in King Arthur's Court* appears on its surface to be a light and humorous adventure story. It is more than that. Mark Twain has written in this novel a parody of medieval English chivalry. (A parody is a humorous imitation.) It is also a parody of medieval English romance. It is an attack on social unfairness and political injustice. It is also an attack on human ignorance. Mark Twain also attacks human superstition.

**Revising Everything
There Is to Revise**

Here is a second revising exercise, this time with parenthetical citations. Use all of your knowledge about revising sentences and about parenthetical documentation to improve these paragraphs. Write your changes directly on the text.

Critics have called Sophocles' ancient Greek tragedy *Oedipus Rex* the first detective story. In *Oedipus Rex*, Oedipus sets out to find the cause of a plague that is killing the people living in his city of Thebes. Oedipus, by the way, I forgot to tell you, is king there. Oedipus consults oracles and prophets, follows clues, tracks down witnesses and interviews them, along the way he discovers that the real mystery he must solve is his own identity. Did you know that in ancient Greece the actors all wore masks? Oedipus resists what he finds out, for his is the story of a "lost one found" (Richmond Lattimore, page 82, of "The Poetry of Greek Tragedy").

The ancient Greek philosopher, whose name was Aristotle, thought that Sophocles' play *Oedipus Rex* was the greatest example of tragedy (Aristotle, *Poetics*, page 36). The play has a hero who struggles against his horrible fate that the gods have decreed even before his birth. No matter what Oedipus and others did to avoid this fate, it follows him. Oscar Brocket says this is an important theme in the play: "man's limitation in controlling his fate" (p. 51). I won't tell you what that fate was because I don't want to ruin the story for you. According to Edith Hamilton in her book *Mythology*, everyone in ancient Greece knew the legend of Oedipus. You can read Sophocles' play or Hamilton's retelling (Hamilton: 256–61)—or both.

Exercise 10 — Revising Sentences in Your Draft

Read through your draft again, focusing this time on individual sentences and on the way sentences work together in a paragraph. Vary the sentence beginnings. Combine some sentences to vary sentence length and structure. Reword, rearrange, and generally improve the sentences in each paragraph. You may want to cut whole sentences or delete words and phrases.

Diction: Choosing the Right Word

☑ **Focus on word choice.**

Your final reading in the revision stage is one of the most important. This time, you will examine word choice, or **diction**.

FIND THE BEST WORD POSSIBLE. BE PRECISE. The English language is very rich in **synonyms**, words that have almost the same meaning. Find and use the word that means exactly what you are trying to say. You can discover the different shades of meaning among synonyms and near-synonyms by checking a good dictionary.

WATCH YOUR TONE. A research paper should be written in formal standard English— that is, without contractions, colloquial expressions, and certainly, slang.

AVOID CLICHÉS. Say it your way. Do not fall into the trap of using clichés— overworked, hackneyed expressions.

Exercise 11 — Focusing on Word Choice

As you revise this introduction to a research paper, focus on word choice. See if you can substitute precise words for vague terms. Revise the paragraph to give it a formal tone, replacing or omitting clichés, contractions, slang, and colloquial expressions. Write your changes directly on the text.

> Chances are pretty good that you probably already know that *Hamlet* by William Shakespeare is a really terrific play. But the really weird thing about the play is that nobody knows for sure exactly what Shakespeare wrote. That's because we don't have the original script written by Shakespeare in his very own handwriting. Guys who are experts on *Hamlet* are pretty sure that the play was written somewhere in the vicinity of 1599 or 1600, and there're three versions that we know about. In 1604, a

version called the Good Quarto was written down a couple of years after *Hamlet*'s opening night. (There's a story, supposed to be true but no one knows for sure, that Shakespeare himself played the Ghost in *Hamlet*. Remember that Shakespeare was an actor before he was a playwright.) An earlier version of *Hamlet* that guys who know a lot call the Bad Quarto is a hacked-up, messed-up version that was published in 1603, but some fools must've lost it and it wasn't found again until 1823. The third version is called the First Folio—now that's confusing, isn't it? The First Folio presents a still different version of *Hamlet* and was published in 1623. This paper will talk about how the three versions of *Hamlet*'re alike and how they're not alike—and check out some ideas about what people who know a lot think about these three versions.

WORKING TOGETHER

Exercise 12 **Revising for Word Choice**

Read through your paper one last time, focusing this time on word choice. Look for places where you can use more-precise words. Eliminate contractions, colloquial expressions, slang, and anything else that detracts from a formal tone. Never use text-message abbreviations. When you have finished revising, exchange papers with a partner. Read each other's papers carefully, then discuss any suggestions for further changes. Explain your reasoning.

Exercise 13 **Checking Your Progress**

Answer each of the following questions about the work you've done so far.

1. How much time have you spent revising your paper?

_____

_____

2. What, if anything, did you change when you focused on unity and on coherence?

_____

_____

3. What kinds of changes did you make in sentence structure and word choice?

_____

_____

4. How satisfied are you that this paper is the best work you can do? Explain.

_____

_____

5. What do you need to do before you are finished?

_____

_____

Checklist Review

Monday
1

Are you on schedule?
Check the Timetables on page 10.

☐ Allow yourself plenty of time to revise.

☐ Read your paper several times, focusing on a different aspect each time.

☐ Check to see that you have met all of your teacher's requirements.

☐ Focus on the paper's unity.

☐ Focus on the paper's coherence.

☐ Focus on each sentence and on the way that related sentences work together.

☐ Focus on word choice.

STEP 9

For more on proofreading, see Step 9 in the two model research papers at **www.sadlierresearchpaper.com**.

Find and Correct Errors

YOU PROBABLY SHOULD START A NEW PARAGRAPH HERE, AND THEN MAYBE CAPITALIZE THIS WORD..

WHAT ELSE WOULD YOU LIKE TO KNOW?

SHOW ME WHERE YOU SPRINKLE IN THE LITTLE CURVY MARKS..

COMMAS WHATEVER

© 1987 United Feature Syndicate, Inc.

11-9

Peanuts Reprinted by permission of USF, Inc.

You are satisfied that the content and style of your paper are as good as you can make them. But your research paper is not quite done. Your final task is to proofread your revised draft for mistakes. When you proofread (or edit) your draft, you will focus on finding and correcting errors in spelling, punctuation, and grammar. Proofreading is much easier than revising, but it still requires your total attention.

Before You Start

You will need ready access to a good college dictionary or an unabridged dictionary and a grammar handbook or a handbook on usage. (See Appendix A, "What Every Research Paper Writer Needs.") You might ask your teacher if he or she has a preference about which dictionary and handbook you should use.

e-writing Remember to use the spell check in your word processing program. (If you have any problems, consult the Help menu.) This tool is especially useful because it may call to your attention errors in spelling that you have overlooked or errors of which you are unaware. Keep in mind, however, that the spell check cannot perform the proofreading task for you. A computer is not—and can never be—a satisfactory substitute for a careful and painstaking reader. For example, if you used *there* instead of *their* or *to* when you meant *too*, the spell check won't catch your mistake.

By the time you get to the proofreading stage, you probably will not have the time (or energy) to read through your paper several times. Most likely, you will read it through once or twice, focusing on everything there is to find during proofreading. So wait until you are awake and alert. (In other words, 3 A.M. the night before your

Proofreader's Symbols

☑ Learn to use the proofreader's symbols.

SYMBOL	MEANING	EXAMPLE
∧	Insert	Cels are the basic units ∧of life.
✗	Delete (remove)	Plant cells have ✗ a wall and chloroplasts.
∽	Delete and close up	An egg is a single cell.
∩	Transpose (switch)	Red ⌐cells⌐ blood ⌐carry oxgyen.
≡	Capitalize	all cells store genetic information in dna.
/	Make lowercase	We studied cells last year in Biology.
#	Add space	When I looked at a drop of pond#water through the microscope, I saw an amoeba.
⌒	Close up space	The study of cell biolog ⌒ y is called "cytology."
¶	Start new paragraph	"Wow! Look at this!" Sue yelled, peering into the microscope.¶"Did you ever see anything so weird-looking?" Martin asked.
⊙	Period	Cells perform many important functions⊙
⌃,	Comma	Plant cells contain chlorophyll⌃,but animal cells do not.
⌃;	Semicolon	Nerve cells transmit messages⌃;muscle cells contract to make movement possible.
⨀	Colon	Most cells have these three things⨀a nucleus, a membrane, and cytoplasm.
=	Hyphen	An amoeba is a one=celled organism that moves by changing its shape.
∨'	Apostrophe	A plant∨'s green color comes from its chlorophyll.
∨" / ∨"	Quotation marks	✗"Your lab reports are due tomorrow,✗"Mrs. Merckel reminded us.

paper is due is not a good time.) Proofread your revised draft, make corrections, and then print out a clean copy.

DO IT YOURSELF. Give yourself enough time to read slowly, *word for word*. If you look quickly through your paper, chances are your eyes will skip right over many mistakes. Slow your reading rate to a crawl, and concentrate. A quiet room and good lighting will help. If a word looks "funny" or sounds strange, consult a dictionary. Check punctuation, grammar, and usage questions in a grammar handbook.

Here are some proofreading techniques to try.

- Read your paper aloud to yourself. This will slow your reading and help you focus on one word at a time.
- Cover the text with a piece of paper, and read only one line at a time. Focus on each word.
- Read the wrong way—from the bottom of a page to the top or from right to left.

WORKING TOGETHER **ANOTHER PAIR OF EYES.** When you have found as many errors as you can, exchange papers with a classmate or two. A peer editor may spot mistakes you have missed.

Spelling

 Check the spelling of words.

Students often complain, "How can I look up a word in a dictionary if I don't know how it's spelled?" Ask a friend or relative, or use your imagination and try several possible spellings. When you track down the correct spelling, be sure to add that word to your proofreading log (see page 142).

WHICH WORD? The English language has many **homonyms**, words that sound the same but have different spellings and meanings (for example, *piece, peace; write, right, rite; it's, its; wear, ware, where; weather, whether*). Make sure that you have used the right word in the right place. That is, make sure you have spelled a word correctly according to its meaning in the sentence.

e-writing A spell check stops at every word not in its dictionary (that includes most names and many other proper nouns) and sometimes makes silly suggestions. On the plus side, however, a spell check will catch *all* typographical errors in words contained in its dictionary, such as *youself* when you meant to type *yourself*. A more serious problem occurs with homonyms. The spell check will not alert you to places where you have used *it's* for *its* or *accept* when you mean *except* or *already* when you mean *all ready*. Even if you use a spell check, you will still have to proofread your paper carefully.

ONE WORD OR TWO? A **compound word** is made up of two or more words working together as a single unit (for example, *high school*, *tabletop*, *ice cream*, *attorney general*, *cheerleader*). Check a dictionary if you are in doubt about whether to spell such words as one word or two.

HYPHENATE OR NOT? Learn the rules for when to hyphenate compound words, and double-check in a dictionary if you are unsure. You will need to hyphenate compound numbers (*thirty-one*), some words beginning with the prefixes *ex-* and *self-* (*ex-president*, *self-confidence*), words ending with the suffix *-elect* (*governor-elect*), and words in which a prefix comes before a capitalized word (*all-American*).

PROPER NAMES. Double-check the spelling of all proper names (author's name, title, publisher, city) in your citations.

- Make sure you have spelled the author's name exactly the way you spelled it on your bibliography source card.
- Make sure the author's name is spelled the same way in your parenthetical citations and the Works Cited list.

> **Hint!**
> Do not hyphenate words at the end of a line unless the word is spelled with a hyphen.

Exercise 1 Proofreading for Spelling Errors

Cross out every word that is spelled incorrectly, and write the word correctly in the space above it.

REM sleep has been shone to have an important conection with dreams. REM, which stands for rapid eye movment, seems to be the sleep period when most or all dreams ocur. During a REM period, the subject's eyes move under closed eyelids, they're is a change in breatheing, and there are distinctive brain wave patterns. A REM period lasts any where from ten to ninty minutes and usually ocurs four to six times a night.

Experiments have been conducted in which patience were deprived of REM sleep. Researches watched the sleeping patience and wakened them as soon as rapid eye movments were visible. Subjects deprived of REM sleep were extremly iritable the next day and acted as if they had recieved very little sleep, even though they had all had their

normal amount of six to ten hours of sleep. After five
nites in a row of REM deprivation, researchers aloud the
subjects REM sleep. One subject's first REM period, which
would normaly last about ten minutes, lasted sixty-eight
minutes. It was as if his body or mind were making up for
the lack of dream sleep on the five previus nights.

Exercise 2 — Checking the Spelling in Your Final Draft

If you have time to read your paper once through just for spelling, do it now. Be especially careful to check the spelling of names used in your citations and Works Cited list.

Exercise 3 — Creating a Personal Proofreading Log

If you do not already have one, start your own personal *proofreading log*, a list of errors you have found in your work. Use the lines below, or write your log on a separate sheet of paper or on your computer. Besides spelling mistakes, record other errors you have caught in proofreading: punctuation, capitalization, grammar, and usage. Save your log for future reference. The next time you write an essay or research paper, review your proofreading log *before* you begin drafting and also when you proofread.

Capitalization

☑ **Make sure you have observed the rules of capitalization.**

START EACH SENTENCE WITH A CAPITAL LETTER.

CAPITALIZE PROPER NOUNS AND PROPER ADJECTIVES. Here are a few examples: Willa Cather, U.S.S. *Missouri*; Cincinnati, Ohio; Norwegian salmon. If in doubt, check a grammar and usage handbook to review the rules of capitalization.

Exercise 4 — Proofreading a Paragraph

Cross out each incorrectly spelled word, and write the correct spelling in the space above it. Use the proofreader's symbols for capitalizing or lowercasing (see page 139).

There are many ways to look at art, and in his poem "Museum piece," the american poet richard wilbur defines three attitudes. in the first stanza, the speaker describes the museum guards as "the good gray gauardians ofart" (1.1). They are ever-present, always hoverinbg about to make sure that nothing happens to any of the valueable Museum peices. They are "impartially protective" (1.3), watching over every peace of Art with equal care, whether or not they agree with there subject matter. Even tho they may be suspicius of the french artist Toulouse-Lautrec (1.4), they protect his paintings with as much attention as they give to anyone else's. The guards don't seem to care weather or not each peace of art is appealing to them. To them, Art is an investment to be watched over as carefuly as one would watch over a fine car or even a pile of money. Their is certainly respect in this atitude, but no love and no feeling for beauty. The whole tone of this first stanza suggests a sort of dull reliability through the use of the adjective *gray* and the description of the spongy, comfortable shoes that are useful for the guards' endless pacing up and down the museums hall ways.

Punctuation

☑ **Read through your paper, and correct any errors in punctuation.**

Indent each new paragraph. Here is a chance to take another look at each paragraph to make sure you haven't combined two paragraphs. Remember to cover each main idea in its own paragraph, complete with paragraph indent and topic sentence.

Make sure each sentence has the appropriate end punctuation mark.

```
Max Planck, a German physicist, developed the quantum

theory, which suggests that light is neither waves nor

particles but has properties of both ("Light" 191) ⊙
                                                    ∧
```

Place a parenthetical citation correctly in relation to punctuation marks.

```
In The Universe in the Light of Modern Physics, Planck

asserts, "We have no right to assume that any physical

laws exist, or if they have existed up to now, that

they will continue to exist in a similar manner in

the future." (393) ⊙
                    ∧
```

Use quotation marks correctly.

```
Albert Einstein, who developed Planck's theories

further, stated in 1930, "The most beautiful thing we

can experience is the mysterious. It is the source of

all true art and science" (Einstein 39).
```

Exercise 5 | **Proofreading Your Final Draft for Punctuation**

As you proofread your final draft, check every punctuation mark. Ask yourself:

- Is each punctuation mark the correct one? (Be especially careful not to mix up colons and semicolons.)
- Are there unnecessary commas? (Take them out.)
- Has necessary punctuation been omitted? (Put it in.)

Add any punctuation errors to your proofreading log, especially if you have made the mistake more than once.

Grammar and Usage

☑ **As you proofread your paper, correct any errors in grammar and usage.**

Check to make sure you have written complete sentences. Avoid sentence fragments and run-on sentences. A complete sentence has a subject and a verb and expresses a complete thought. If any of these items is missing, you have written a sentence fragment.

> _travels_
> Light ∧ ~~traveling~~ at about 186,000 miles per second.

A run-on sentence has two or more complete sentences written as one sentence. A run-on sentence may have no punctuation or only a comma separating what should be two (or even more) sentences.

> Sound travels faster when air temperatures are warm⊙
> for example, at 20 degrees Centigrade, sound travels
> about 40 ft. per second faster than at 0° Centigrade.

Check to see that each verb agrees with its subject.

> Both the whale and the dolphin communicates by means
> of underwater sounds.

Check to see that the antecedent of every pronoun is absolutely clear.

> The lens and cornea are important parts at the front
> _They_
> of the eye. ∧ ~~It~~ focuses light on the retina at the
> back of the eye.

WORKING TOGETHER | **Exercise 6** | **What Is Wrong with These Sentences?**

Fix every mistake you find. Then, on a separate sheet of paper or on your computer, rewrite each sentence correctly. Get together with a partner to compare your corrected sentences. What, if anything, did you miss? Add these mistakes to your proofreading log.

1. Henry David Thoreau, one of americas leading philosophers were a freind of Ralph Waldo Emerson, the essayist and poet.

2. In 1845 Thoreau built a small wooden cabin on the shore of Walden pond and he lived their for almost too years.

3. Of course one of the reasons he went to walden pond was to experience it's incredible beauty which he describes in *Walden* his book is based on the very detailed journal he kept while he lived in his cabin.

4. Thoreau had deeper motives tham merely appreication of natures beauty he believed as Emerson did that nature reflects the inner self and teaches us much about life.

5. In Walden Thoreau tells of meeting a poor woodcutter who had very few material things but posessed a love of nature and was honest simple and content

6. The essayist E B White called Walden "the only book I own". White said that he kept Thoreaus book handy "for relief" during times of despair.

7. In the conclusion to Walden, Thoreau wrote, If a man does not keep pace with his companions, perhaps it is becuase he hears a different drummer Let him step to the music which he hears, however measured or far away.

8. Thoreau also wrote these wrods: "if one advances confidently in the direction of his dreams, and endevors to live the life which he has imagined, he will meet with a succes unexpected in common hours

9. Thoreau's essay "Civil disobedience," which he published in 1849 explained why he refused to pay the Massachusets poll tax.

10. Both Mahatma Gandhi leader of India's struggle for independence from britain, and Dr. Martin luther king, jr. American civil rights leader was inspired by this essay

Documentation

☑ Check your parenthetical citations against your Works Cited list.

- Every work you have mentioned in a parenthetical citation should have a corresponding entry in the Works Cited list.
- Every entry on the Works Cited list should have at least one parenthetical citation in your paper.
- Double-check to make sure the entries in the Works Cited list are in alphabetical order.

WORKING TOGETHER

 Exercise 7 Proofreading Your Final Draft

Proofread your entire paper once more, this time focusing on capitalization, grammar and usage, and documentation. Correct any mistakes you find, add them to your proofreading log, and print your paper. If you have time, find a partner, and proofread each other's final drafts.

Exercise 8 Proofreading One Last Time

Don't turn in your final paper without another round of proofreading. You want to make sure that no new errors have crept in as you have made corrections. Read it one more time. (If possible, let some time elapse between the two readings.)

Exercise 9 Checking Your Progress

Answer each of the following questions about the work you have done so far.

1. What kinds of mistakes did you catch when you were proofreading your paper?

   _____

   _____

2. Are you finished? If so, hooray! If not, what do you still have left to do?

   _____

   _____

3. What have you learned about yourself and your writing habits?

   _____

   _____

4. What will you do differently next time you write a research paper?

_____

_____

5. What are the strongest parts of your paper? What are the weakest parts?

_____

_____

Checklist Review

Monday 1 — Are you on schedule? Check the Timetables on page 10.

- ☐ Learn to use the proofreader's symbols.
- ☐ As you proofread, check the spelling of words.
- ☐ Double-check the spelling of all proper names (author's name, title, publisher, city) in your citations.
- ☐ Make sure that you have observed the rules of capitalization.
- ☐ Check for errors in punctuation.
- ☐ Correct any errors in grammar and usage.
- ☐ Check your parenthetical citations against your Works Cited list.

For more on publishing your research, see Step 10 in the two model research papers at **www.sadlierresearchpaper.com.**

Publish Your Research

YES, I KNOW MY TERM PAPER IS DUE TOMORROW.

OH, YES, MA'AM, I'M ALMOST FINISHED...

THE *TITLE*?

...I CALL IT... "WORK IN PROGRESS."

© 1990 Tribune Media Services, Inc. All Rights Reserved

Reprinted by permission: Tribune Media Services

Congratulations! You have kept plugging away at this monumental task, one step at a time. The hardest parts are behind you. Now you have only two things left to do: reprinting your final paper and proofreading it one last time. If you have followed one of the suggested timetables on page 10, you should have plenty of time to finish before your due date. Don't try to finish your paper the night before it is due. If you wait until the last minute, something is sure to go wrong. Allow at least two days so that if disaster strikes on the first day, you will still be able to finish on time. Check to see that the equipment (computer, printer) you plan to use is working and that you have on hand everything you can possibly need. Having a printer cartridge run out of ink or toner is a last-minute nightmare.

Ways to Publish Your Research

To complete your assignment, you will probably have to turn in a written report, so follow the guidelines on pages 152–153 for producing the final version of your research paper. You also might consider sharing your research in one of the following alternate publishing forms. **Important:** Don't get started on any of these projects until your teacher has approved your plan.

☑ Multimedia Report

Suppose you're writing about the new panda in a local zoo, and you've interviewed one of the zookeepers about it. How can you share with your audience what you've learned from this interview?

VIDEO. With a camcorder, a digital camera, a cell phone, or the movie-making software on a computer, you can create a **video** of all or part of your interview. You can insert your homemade video into your research paper (if submitting a digital copy of your document), or you can show it as part of an oral presentation. A homemade video would also make a useful addition to an oral history report or a report on a historic place. For step-by-step instructions on how to create a video, carefully read the manual that came with the equipment or software, or talk to someone who knows how.

If you want to use a ready-made video you've found online, be sure to give full credit to your source in your Works Cited list. Here's how to insert an online video into your research paper. Carefully type the full URL into your report. It will turn blue and become a **hyperlink**, so a reader who double-clicks on the link can access the Web site and watch the video.

PRESENTATION SOFTWARE. You can create multimedia presentations on your computer that can later be displayed in the classroom on a computer, a TV screen, or a whiteboard. A "slide show" (a series of photographs or other graphics) can highlight your research, with images, charts, videos, and animation. Learn how to use these programs by studying the detailed online tutorials provided by their makers or by searching the Internet using the term "presentation software in the classroom."

Your slide show should be directly related to the topic of your research paper. As you show each slide, tell your audience what it is seeing, and give additional information about the graphic or its subject.

The graphics should highlight important aspects of your topic. For a presentation on "Women's Contributions to the Civil War," for instance, a combination of photographs, bulleted lists, and charts can serve as eye-pleasing tools for conveying information. In the example below, one slide includes a picture of the Union spy Mary Bowser and several bulleted items that emphasize pivotal moments in her life. Another slide features a graph that presents data on women's participation in the war.

Mary Bowser (1839–?)

• Servant and spy in home of Confederate leader Jefferson Davis

• Presumed illiterate, she read military plans and eavesdropped while serving tea

• Passed information to Thomas McNiven, the town baker, who headed Richmond's spy network

• Under suspicion, Bowser fled Virginia near the end of the war and was never heard from again

Sources:
Gates, Henry Louis, and Evelyn Brooks Higginbotham, eds. *African American National Biography*, Harvard University. 9 Oct. 2009. Web. <http://www.fas.harvard.edu/~aanb/SHTML/DOWNLOADS/Sample%20entries%20for%20Web%20site.pdf>.

Some Roles for Women in the Civil War

Number of Women

Spies[1]   Soldiers[2]   Nurses[3]

Sources:
1. The National Civil War Museum, Harrisburg, PA.
2. Livermore, Mary A. *My Story of the War.* Hartford, CT: A.D. Worthington and Company, 1888. pp. 119–20. Print.
3. Civil War Home. Web. 9 February 2010. <http://www.civilwarhome.com/civilwarnurses.htm>.

All numbers are estimates.

☑ Oral Presentation

Your teacher may encourage you to present the content of your research paper in a speaking-listening situation.

INFORMAL SPEECH. Instead of reading your whole paper aloud, present your report using notes or your final outline to help you remember your main ideas. As you speak, you might also use visuals (charts, diagrams, videos, or posters) to present factual information.

Q & A. After your oral presentation, spend five minutes or so on a **Q & A**, a question-and-answer session. Encourage your audience to ask questions about your research, your sources, and your conclusions. Remember that you're the local expert on the topic you've researched, so feel confident that you know much more about your research topic than anyone else in the class.

PANEL DISCUSSION. If two or more students have written about the same issue or problem, present a panel discussion to discuss your research and your conclusions. Meet beforehand to identify and organize the main discussion topics. Designate one person as the moderator. The moderator's job is to introduce the panelists and the topic and to keep the discussion going smoothly.

DEBATE. If you've written about a problem-solution topic (perhaps an issue your school or community is facing, or something you feel needs changing), consider holding a debate. Get together with other students to argue both sides of the issue, presenting relevant background information and facts, as well as the opinions of experts. Clearly state your own opinion and conclusions as well, using your research to support your position. Treat the opposition's views respectfully as you present your **counterarguments** (logical arguments aimed at defeating the opposing view).

POSTER. At conventions, presenters make large posters that summarize their research. These visuals help speakers deliver their message. Think about how you might "sum up" your research in a single poster. What information or graphics might you use? How would you present your thesis, your main ideas, and your conclusion? To support your presentation, you might want to create a poster, present it to the class, and answer any questions about it.

TELL THE OUTSIDE WORLD. Is your research about a topic or issue that local government or school officials might be interested in? Is there a school or community group directly or indirectly related to your topic? Send a copy of your paper along with a cover letter offering to present your research to the group.

Hint!

You can find out anything you need to know about creating a multimedia presentation by typing a question into a search engine—for example, "How can I insert a video into a Word document?"

☑ Written Report

You may choose to present your research in writing.

PAMPHLET OR BROCHURE. Use a desktop publishing program to create a 4- or 8-page pamphlet on your topic. (Search the Help feature for a built-in template that comes with some software.) If you researched careers in Health Services or Information Technology or if you wrote about what makes the Galapagos Islands unique, how would you share your information in an easy-to-read format? Study magazines and travel brochures to analyze how their designs help convey information and persuade the reader.

WEB SITE OR BLOG. If your school has a Web site and your teacher and the school's media specialist approve, post your paper on it. Or you might post your paper online as part of a blog or on a personal or family Web page. To learn how to create your own blog, use a search engine for the phrase "free blog publishing tool."

  Think About Different Formats

Work with a partner to brainstorm ideas about how and where you might publish your research. What formats other than the traditional written paper might work best. Why? On the lines below, list the equipment you would need, and write notes on how you would go about finding out what you'd need to know.

_____

_____

_____

The Paper's Form

☑ Follow the format that your teacher requires.

If your teacher has not specified any special requirements, follow these standard conventions:

PAPER. Use 8 1/2" x 11" white paper. Print on only one side of each piece of paper.

PRINT. A computer's printer should produce a dark copy that is easy to read.

---

e-writing Choose a font and text size that are readable, and stick to them. You are not doing desktop publishing, so do not be tempted to add banner heads and fancy fonts. Keep the text plain, simple, and neat. Remember that the latest MLA style uses italic type (no longer underscore) for book and magazine titles.

DOUBLE-SPACE. Set your word-processing program to double-space, and double-space the entire paper, including all quotations and the Works Cited page.

RUNNING HEAD. On every page, place a running head at the upper-right corner 1/2 inch from the top of the page and 1 inch from the right-hand edge of the paper. The running head consists of your last name followed by the page number. (See the model papers.)

HEADING. The first page of your research paper has a four-line heading that lists your name, your teacher's name, the course title, and the paper's due date. Place the heading 1 inch from the top of the page. It is flush left (aligned with the left-hand margin) and above the title.

TITLE. Center the title above the text. If you have a subheading, be sure to use a colon. Do not underscore or italicize the title or enclose it in quotation marks.

MARGINS. Most word-processing applications set the margins automatically. If yours does not, use 1-inch margins at the top, bottom, and sides of your paper.

INDENTATION. Each paragraph is indented 1/2 inch (5 spaces) from the left margin. In your Works Cited list, indent each turnover line 1/2 inch, too. Long quotations set off as blocks are indented 1 full inch (10 spaces).

HYPHENATION. Do not hyphenate words at the end of a line.

PAGE BREAKS. Make sure you have at least two lines of a paragraph at the bottom of a page and also at the top of a page. This may require some juggling and/or short pages, but do not have single words or lines sitting by themselves. (These are called *widows* if at the top of a page, *orphans* if at the bottom.)

TITLE PAGE. Usually, a title page is not required. If your teacher asks for a title page, however, follow his or her specifications for content and spacing.

GET IT ALL TOGETHER. Find out how your teacher wants you to put your paper together. A paper clip in the upper-left-hand corner is the easiest solution. Do not use a staple, pin, binder, or folder unless your teacher tells you to.

Last but Not Least

☑ **Proofread your final manuscript one last time.**
Be sure not to turn in your final paper until you have read through it one last time, because you want to make sure that no new errors have crept in.

☑ **Make a copy.**
Before you turn in your paper, make a copy for yourself—just in case. You have worked so hard and so long that you should have a copy anyway.

SAMPLE STUDENT RESEARCH PAPERS

The following papers use the MLA style of documentation. A Works Cited list appears at the end of each paper.

SAMPLE PAPER 1

Nardoia 1

Gina Nardoia
Mr. Hugh B. Corlett
English I, Period 2
March 25, 2010

The History and Production of Chocolate

Carolus Linnaeus, a Swedish botanist, classified more than 4,400 species of animals and 7,700 species of plants ("Linnaeus"). In 1753, he named the cacao tree *Theobroma cacao. Theobroma* in Greek means "food of the gods" (Burleigh [ch. 2]). From the pods of this rain forest tree come cacao beans, the raw material of chocolate. Chocolate has a long history as a highly prized food.

The History of Chocolate

We owe chocolate to the ancient civilizations of the New World. More than three thousand years ago, the Olmec people grew cacao trees in the tropical forests of the Amazon River valley and in the foothills of the Andes (Presilla 10). Later, the Maya (who were at the height of their power from AD 300 to AD 900) continued making *tchocolatl*, a bitter drink, from the seeds of the cacao tree ("Maya").

Can you imagine a bitter, gritty chocolate drink flavored with hot chili peppers and topped with foam? That is how the Maya consumed chocolate ("All About Chocolate"). To the Maya and to the Aztecs after them, chocolate was a precious drink. It was used in religious ceremonies and was considered so important that only kings, nobles, priests, and warriors were allowed to drink it (Presilla 14–15).

Annotations (right margin):

- Running head 1/2 inch from top of paper; 1-inch margins at top, sides and bottom
- 4-line heading: Name/Teacher/Class/Due date
- Title (centered)
- Introductory paragraph begins with attention-getting facts
- Chapter citation of a source with no page numbers
- Thesis statement
- Subhead (optional)
- Topic sentence
- History of chocolate told in chronological order
- Author's name and page number for book in Works Cited list
- Attention-getting question as topic sentence
- Citation of two pages in a source

In 1502, Christopher Columbus became the first European to sample chocolate. By that time, cacao seeds had become so valuable to the Aztecs that they were used as money. "A turkey, for example, was worth a hundred seeds. A small rabbit was worth thirty" (Burleigh [ch. 1]). Even taxes could be paid with cacao seeds.

In 1519, Hernándo Cortés, the Spanish soldier and explorer, came to Mexico searching for gold. Montezuma II, the Aztec emperor, served Cortés and his men *chocolatl* ("bitter water") in special goblets, or glasses, made of gold (Jones 6). Cortés called chocolate "the divine drink which builds up resistance and fights fatigue" (qtd. in Burleigh [ch. 2]). Recognizing its value, he shipped cacao seeds to Spain.

A breakthrough occurred when "an inventive cook in the kitchen of Spain's Queen Isabella I added sugar instead of hot peppers, creating a delicious brew made of roasted, crushed cocoa beans whipped up with hot water or milk, sweetened with sugar or honey, and flavored with vanilla, cinnamon, or other spices" (Beach 2). Spain monopolized the chocolate trade until about 1580. In that year, a chocolate-processing plant opened in Spain. After that, the secret of chocolate gradually spread across Europe; and the Dutch, French, British, Portuguese, and Germans started cacao plantations in their tropical colonies.

Only wealthy Europeans could afford the hot, frothy, sweetened drink (Presilla 20). It was served in beautiful, specially made china cups (Beach 3). In England, there were many chocolate houses, where wealthy men went to drink cocoa, discuss ideas, and gossip with their friends (Jones

Topic sentence

Specific example

Events told in chronological order, with many "time words" to clarify

Historical quote found in a secondary source

Direct quotation from a book

Topic sentence

7). Samuel Pepys, the English writer, noted in his diary in 1664: "To a coffee house, to drink jocolatte, very good" (qtd. in Burleigh [ch. 2]).

Historical quote found in secondary source

In 1765, cocoa beans were exported to the American colonies, and chocolate soon became a popular drink.

Topic sentence

Twenty-two-year-old Thomas Jefferson praised chocolate as "superior to coffee or tea for health and nourishment" (Beach 3). In the colonies, however, there were no chocolate houses. Wealthy Americans drank their chocolate at home. Also, "chocolate was generally marketed to the masses rather than the elite (as in Europe), with the emphasis on wholesomeness rather than sophistication" (McFadden and France 23). In this way, chocolate became popular with everyone.

Source with two authors

Throughout its history, chocolate had been a drink. But in the nineteenth century, there were new developments. In 1828, a Dutch chemist named Coenraad Van Houten invented a press that separated the cocoa butter (the fat) from the cacao beans. The hard, dry cakes of chocolate that were left could easily be crushed into cocoa powder (McFadden and France 16). Then in 1847, an important change occurred. An English chocolate maker, J. S. Fry, combined cocoa powder, sugar, and cocoa butter to make the first solid chocolate. Chocolate could be eaten as well as sipped! In 1876, a Swiss chocolate maker named Daniel Peter discovered how to add milk to chocolate, and the first milk chocolate was manufactured (Jones 7).

Topic sentence

How Chocolate Is Produced

Subhead (optional)

Chocolate may grow on trees, but it is a long, laborious process from the tree to a candy bar. Cacao trees grow in

Topic sentence

tropical forests, where they are shaded by taller trees.
They have small, five-petaled flowers that develop into long
pods on the branches and trunk. David Bar-Zvi, a curator of
tropical plants at Fairchild Tropical Gardens in Miami, says
that a cacao tree begins producing pods when it is only
4 or 5 feet high but grows to 30 feet or more. The pods
vary in shape and color. Some look like deflated footballs
with bumpy skins. Others are smoother and more oval in
shape. Unripe pods are green, but they change to yellow or
purple-red when they ripen (Burleigh [ch. 1]).

Workers cut the ripe pods from the tall trees—no easy
task. Then they split the pods open with a machete. Inside
is a gooey white pulp covering rows of almond-sized seeds—
some 20—40 seeds to a pod (Presilla 10). Workers pile the
seeds and pulp into heaps and cover them with banana leaves
to ferment. After about six days, the seeds are spread out
to dry in the sun. Gradually, they darken from tan or white
or light pink to dark brown, and then they are packed in
bags and sold (McFadden and France 32—33).

The next steps in the chocolate-making process are
roasting the dried seeds and removing the husks. Then the
seeds are crushed to a smooth paste (Presilla 18). In modern
chocolate factories, other steps are added. The paste is
conched (gently stirred in big machines) and tempered
(slowly cooled) to increase flavor and smoothness (Jones
13—14).

The Benefits of Chocolate

Many people who eat or drink chocolate say that it makes
them feel happy (Kuwana). Cortés and Jefferson believed
that chocolate was not only tasty but also healthy. Over

Personal interview with an expert; appositive identifies expert

Factual details

Description of a process, told in chronological order

Parenthetical definitions of unfamiliar terms

Subhead (optional)

Source of idea

the centuries, others have praised chocolate as a cure for all kinds of ailments. Now some scientists think chocolate may indeed be good for you. Cocoa contains antioxidant substances called "flavonoids." Antioxidants "may help decrease blood pressure and improve circulation" (Olson). More studies will be necessary before we know whether eating or drinking chocolate really does contribute to good health.

Chocolate may also have a role to play in saving some of the world's endangered rain forests. Cacao trees thrive only in the moist and shady tropical forests that are threatened by logging and farming. If this valuable crop can be grown in shady, regenerating forests without the use of pesticides and fertilizers, and if it can yield good profits and wages to growers and workers, it may be possible to make saving forests economically attractive (Bright).

So the next time you bite into a chocolate bar or drink a steaming mug of cocoa, stop to think about the long history of chocolate, the people who work to grow and process cacao beans, and the things we still have to learn about this delicious food.

Topic sentence in the middle of the paragraph

Direct quotation from a newspaper article

Topic sentence

Concluding paragraph

Nardoia 6

Works Cited

"All About Chocolate: History of Chocolate." *Chocolate: The
     Exhibition*. 2002. The Field Museum. Web. 3 Nov. 2004.
     <http://www.fmnh.org/chocolate/history_intro.html>.

Bar-Zvi, David. Personal interview. 8 Nov. 2004.

Beach, Neva. *The Ghirardelli Chocolate Cookbook*. Berkeley:
     Ten Speed Press, 1995. Print.

Bright, Chris. "Chocolate Could Bring the Forest Back."
     World Watch Nov./Dec. 2001: 17–28. Worldwatch Institute.
     Web. 3 Nov. 2004. <http://www.worldwatch.org/>.

Burleigh, Robert. *Chocolate: Riches from the Rainforest*. New
     York: Abrams, 2002. N. pag. Print.

Jones, Carol. *From Farm to You: Chocolate*. Philadelphia:
     Chelsea House, 2003. Print.

Kuwana, Ellen. "The Complexities of Chocolate." *Neuroscience
     for Kids* 20 Dec. 2000. Eric H. Chudler. Web. 3 Nov. 2004.
     <http://faculty.washington.edu/chudler/nchoc.html>.

"Linnaeus, Carolus." *The Columbia Encyclopedia*. 6th ed. 2001.
     Print.

"Maya." *The Columbia Encyclopedia*. 6th ed. 2001. Print.

McFadden, Christine, and Christine France. *Chocolate:
     Cooking with the World's Best Ingredient*. London:
     Hermes House, 2003. Print.

Olson, Elizabeth. "Beyond Delicious, Chocolate May Help Pump
     Up Your Heart." *New York Times* 17 Feb. 2004: D5+. Print.

Presilla, Maricel E. *The New Taste of Chocolate: A Cultural and
     Natural History of Cacao with Recipes*. Berkeley: Ten Speed
     Press, 2001. Print.

Start new page; center title 1 inch from top of paper

Indent turnover lines 1/2 inch

Personal interview with local expert

Date of access and Web site URL

N. pag. means "no pagination"

Colon separates title and subtitle

Article from online newsletter

Unsigned encyclopedia article

Book with two authors; second author listed with first name followed by last name

Newspaper article

Washington 1

Benjamin Washington
Ms. Applegate
English III, Period 4
March 31, 2010

Lacrosse: Yesterday and Today

If you go to a lacrosse game today, you will see a
fast-moving, rough sport that resembles soccer, ice hockey,
and football. Like hockey, lacrosse is a stick-and-ball game
in which players manipulate the ball/puck without touching
it with their hands. As in hockey and soccer, players try
to score points by advancing the ball/puck past a defending
goalie and into the opposing team's net-shaped goal. As in
all three sports, players struggle fiercely to prevent their
opponents from scoring. Like all three sports, lacrosse is
an aggressive game with teams charging up and down a field.
However, as exciting as it is to watch or play lacrosse
today, it cannot compare with the earliest games of
lacrosse played by Native Americans.

A Native American Game

Imagine a game that lasts three days with hundreds,
sometimes thousands, of players racing up and down a
playing field that has no set boundaries. The field might
be as long as three miles and as wide as a mile. Play stops
at sunset but is resumed at sunrise. It is said that some
players die of exhaustion (Taylor).

We have a good idea of what American Indian lacrosse
looked like from the paintings and drawings of George
Catlin (1796–1872). Catlin documented Native American life
during his travels in the West from the 1830s to 1850s. In

Running head
1/2 inch from top
of paper; 1-inch
margins at top,
sides, and bottom

4-line heading:
Name/Teacher/
Class/Due date

Title (centered);
colon separates
broad subject and
limited focus

Introductory
paragraph
compares lacrosse
with three
familiar sports

Transitional word

Thesis statement

Subhead (optional)

Attention-getting
introduction to
history of lacrosse

Topic sentence

Catlin's *Ball Play of the Choctaw—Ball Up, 1834–1835*, we
see a melee on the field with more than a hundred players,
some wrestling each other to the ground (Hoyt-Goldsmith
12–13). One team has used white body paint to distinguish
itself from the other team, and each player carries two
lacrosse sticks. (In *Lacrosse: A History of the Game*,
Donald Fisher notes that in the Northeast and around the
Great Lakes, players used a single long stick but that in
the Southeast players used a pair of shorter sticks [13]).

In Catlin's painting, the players wear only loincloths
with decorative tails made of horsehair attached to their
backs. They wear feathers in their hair, and their feet
are bare. According to Hoyt-Goldsmith, players wore animal
charms, such as a hawk feather or bear claw, so that the
animal's spirit would help them during a game (15).

Catlin shows the game being played in a beautiful green,
flat field with hills in the background and spectators
on the sidelines. The goalpost—a horizontal sapling tied
across the tops of two tall saplings—looks like today's
football goalposts.

Lacrosse is a traditional game that has been played in
the Americas for centuries. Perhaps it is a descendant of
the stick-and-ball games played in ancient Mayan and Aztec
cultures (Nicholson 11). The game, which the Iroquois
called *guh-chee-gwuh-ai*, "was part of the Indians' religious
beliefs. Whether Algonquin or Iroquois, Cherokee or Creek,
Sioux or Santee, all believed that the Creator gave them
the game for a special purpose" (Hoyt-Goldsmith 11).

The earliest written descriptions of lacrosse come from
the diaries of French Jesuit missionaries, who came to
the New World in the 1600s to try to convert the Native

Americans to Christianity. While living among the Hurons near Thunder Bay, Ontario, Father François Joseph Le Mercier reported that clans played a series of lacrosse games to bring good weather for the newly planted seed corn (Vennum 12).

Another reason to play lacrosse was to cure the sick. Father Jean de Brébeuf wrote in 1637:

> There is a poor sick man, fevered of body and almost dying, and a miserable Sorcerer will order for him, as a cooling remedy, a game of crosse. Or the sick man himself, sometimes, will have dreamed that he must die unless the whole country shall play crosse for his health; and, no matter how little may be his credit, you will see then in a beautiful field, Village contending against Village, as to who will play crosse the better, and betting against one another Beaver robes and Porcelain collars, so as to excite greater interest. (qtd. in Fisher 17)

The American Indians also used lacrosse to settle disputes between tribes, choosing a brutal game instead of war. Fisher notes that "a contest permitted tribes to reinforce political fellowship while solving territorial disputes within the context of an alliance" (14). The winner of the game won the dispute.

Because lacrosse requires great strength, skill, and endurance, its most important use was to train young men as warriors and hunters (Fisher 13). Southeastern tribes called the game "little brother of war" (Vennum xii).

According to Oren Lyons, a member of the Turtle Clan of the Onondaga Nation and all-American lacrosse player at Syracuse University:

A reason why American Indians played lacrosse

Second reason

Colon introduces long quote

Long historical quote found in secondary source; *qtd in* **means "quoted in"**

Topic sentence; third reason

Direct quote from book

Fourth, most important reason

Contemporary player talks about why American Indians play lacrosse

> Lacrosse has been in our life forever. The first
> mention of it is in 1600 by one of the Jesuit
> priests, talking about the game, but we were playing
> it long before they were here. The first purpose
> of the game is as a "medicine" game played for the
> health and welfare of the people. We still do that.
> It was played for the Creator, to entertain the
> Creator. Any person in the community can call for a
> game, and then immediately the whole society . . .
> creates the game. There's a whole process to it. It's
> a ceremony that requires the correct procedures and
> so forth. (Dellinger)

Lacrosse has always had a spiritual element for Native
Americans. Players fasted, prayed, and underwent a ritual
purification before a game. After a game, both teams went
down to a body of living water, dipped their lacrosse
sticks into the water, and said more ancient prayers.
In *American Indian Lacrosse: Little Brother of War*, Vennum
writes:

> The Jesuits appear to have been aware that a
> lacrosse match was a highly ceremonialized religious
> expression—that the players were required to undergo
> ritual cleansing before and after the sport, that the
> game's outcome was believed to be predetermined by
> spirits, and that success or failure was attributable
> less to athletic prowess than to the relative power
> of the religious leaders who controlled players and
> games at every turn. (28)

The medicine men, or shamans, determined when games
would be played, and they directed the strategies. They
were something like today's coaches (Vennum 28) except that

Long quote, indented and set off; no quotation marks

Source of direct quote

Topic sentence

Title and author mentioned in text

This paper has too many long quotes

Page reference only

Topic sentence

Source of idea

they had—or claimed to have—magical powers. In fact, a lacrosse match among the Eastern Cherokee was seen as a match between each team's medicine man: "And the victory or defeat is laid at the door of the medicine man rather than that the players themselves are congratulated or scorned for it" (Vennum 28).

Only the men played lacrosse. Women cheered their team from the sidelines and were known to whip players if they were not aggressive enough. One Catlin drawing shows a woman with a small branch chasing a player on the field. Catlin explains that she is "'yelling and screaming' as she runs, trying to overtake her husband to remind him of all the goods they have wagered on the game" (Vennum 156–57).

Much was at stake in a game. Players and tribal members placed bets (possessions such as a tool or weapon or article of clothing) on their own team. The winning team divided the spoils among the bettors. "Although a man might lose possessions after betting on one contest, . . . he stood a good chance to recover his losses later" (Fisher 16).

Canada's National Game

Canadians popularized lacrosse and took it over (Taylor). The French in Canada had named the sport *lacrosse* because the lacrosse sticks, curved at one end, resemble the crosier, or staff, of a bishop ("Lacrosse," *Americana*). The Montreal Lacrosse Club, founded in 1856, made lacrosse a game for white gentlemen, who very occasionally played against their Mohawk neighbors (Fisher 25).

William George Beers, a Canadian dentist, is known as the "father of modern lacrosse." Beers played lacrosse as a teenager and was a devoted fan and promoter of the game. In

Topic sentence

Topic sentence

Subhead (optional)

History of modern lacrosse given in chronological order, with many "time words" to clarify

Specifies which of two articles enitled "Lacrosse"

Topic sentence; details that follow explain why Beers is an important figure in modern lacrosse

1869, he published a book of lacrosse rules in an attempt to "stabilize the erratic nature [of the game], and eliminate the petty squabbles over technicalities that inhibited the game" (Mirra). Beers lobbied to make lacrosse Canada's national sport, and on the same day that Canada became a dominion, July 1, 1867, lacrosse was declared its official sport (Hoyt-Goldsmith 15; "Lacrosse," *Columbia*).

> Parenthetical reference with two sources

   Slowly, the popularity of lacrosse in North America grew. The game reached New York City by 1868, when a *New York Tribune* reporter wrote, "Lacrosse may be called a madman's game, so wild it is" (Nicholson 33). Intercollegiate lacrosse in the Northeast began in the fall of 1877. Canadians who settled in the northeastern states founded lacrosse clubs in Baltimore, Boston, and Philadelphia (Fisher 57).

> Topic sentence

   As lacrosse became more popular, Native Americans were prevented from competing. Oren Lyons, honorary chairman of the Iroquois Nationals lacrosse team, remembers:

> Topic sentence

> But I should mention that in 1890 the Iroquois were sanctioned against playing at all. Before that we were always part of the international games. We taught the English how to play, we taught the French how to play, we taught the Canadians and the Americans. We were quite active in the late 1800s. We had three trips to England, played in front of Queen Victoria, and they couldn't beat us so they called us professionals and wouldn't allow us to play anymore. (Dellinger)

> Long direct quote; paper should not have four such long quotes.

Not until 1987 did the International Lacrosse Federation accept the Iroquois people as a full member nation. When they compete in international tournaments, the team members travel with passports of the Haudenosaunee Nation (the Iroquois name for their people) (Dellinger).

> Parenthetical explanation

— Topic sentence

And slowly, very slowly, women took up the game. The first woman's lacrosse association was established in England in 1912 (Nicholson 33). British women teaching in Baltimore, Philadelphia, and New York introduced the game and formed women's lacrosse clubs. The United States Women's Lacrosse Association was formed in 1931, with the first women's championship played in 1933 (Nicholson 37).

The Game Today ——— Subhead (optional)

Youth lacrosse (for players under 15) is growing each — Facts and statistics about lacrosse today
year. (See Table 1.) There are boys teams and girls teams — Reference to table below
in middle schools, high schools, and colleges throughout the United States, not just in the Northeast, where lacrosse first became popular (Tanton). The National Federation of High Schools reports that more than 1,800 high schools have boys lacrosse teams, and more than 1,600 high schools have girls teams (Aungst). At the college level, intercollegiate lacrosse is growing for both men and women ("About Lacrosse").

— Table with information that supports a claim in the text

Table 1.

Number of High School Lacrosse Players in the United States

Year	Boys	Girls	Total
2007	119,826	81,424	201,250
2006	101,667	67,958	169,625

Number of Youth Lacrosse (Under 15) Players in the United States

Year	Boys	Girls	Total
2007	155,866	85,715	241,581
2006	139,188	81,609	220,797

Source: *US Lacrosse* Member Participation Survey 2007.

Lacrosse is played internationally in more than ——— **Topic sentence**
twenty-five nations. There are World Tournaments as well
as Under-19 World Tournaments for players younger than 19.
According to Bill Tanton, senior associate editor of
Lacrosse Magazine, "There are [two professional] men's
leagues, one for indoor lacrosse (also known as box
lacrosse), one for outdoor." Indoor or box lacrosse is
played in ice hockey arenas on artificial turf.

The size of a lacrosse field and the rules and equipment ——— **Facts about women's rules and equipment**
are different for women's lacrosse, but the game is just as
frenetic. Women do not use body checks, as men do, so there
is less violence and no need for padded equipment ("Women's ——— **Transitional word**
Lacrosse" 82–83).

Although the Iroquois team still plays with traditional
wooden sticks handmade from hickory wood and carefully
shaped (Hoyt-Goldsmith 22–25), most players today use ——— **Source cited near information rather than at end of sentence**
titanium lacrosse sticks (Taylor).

For sports enthusiasts all over the world, lacrosse is ——— **Concluding paragraph**
an exciting game to watch or play. Although it has undergone
many changes in its long history, it is still based on
traditional values. If you've never seen a lacrosse game or
played one, search for lacrosse on television or in your ——— **Call to action**
community. You won't regret it, for lacrosse is never boring.

Works Cited

"About Lacrosse." *US Lacrosse*. Web. 3 Mar. 2009.
    <http://www.lacrosse.org/the_sport/index.phtml>

Aungst, Colleen. Message to the author. 3 Mar. 2009. E-mail.

Dellinger, Laura M. "Asserting Sovereignty Through Sports;
    Iroquois Lacrosse Teams Compete Internationally Using
    Tribal Passports." *The Native Voice* 25 Jul. 2003. sec.
    D: 4. *ProQuest*. Miami-Dade Public Lib. Web. 28 Feb.
    2009. <http://mdpls.org/>.

Fisher, Donald M. *Lacrosse: A History of the Game*.
    Baltimore: Johns Hopkins UP, 2002. Print.

Hoyt-Goldsmith, Diane. *Lacrosse: The National Game of the
    Iroquois*. New York: Holiday House, 1998. Print.

"Lacrosse." *The Columbia Encyclopedia*. 6th ed. 2001. Print.

"Lacrosse." *Encyclopedia Americana*. 2001 ed. Print.

Mirra, Gerald B. "American Indian Lacrosse." *Whispering Wind*
    31 Oct. 1998: 20. *ProQuest*. Miami-Dade Public Lib.
    Web. 27 Feb. 2009. <http://mdpls.org/>.

Nicholson, Lois. *The Composite Guide to Lacrosse*.
    Philadelphia: Chelsea House, 1999. Print.

Tanton, Bill. Message to the author. 16 Feb. 2009. E-mail.

Taylor, Drew Hayden. "The Irony Hangs Thick at a Game of
    Lacrosse." *Wind Speaker* Jun. 2002: 5. *General
    Reference Center Gold*. Miami-Dade Public Lib. Web.
    28 Feb. 2009. <http://mdpls.org/>.

Annotations:
- Start new page; center title 1 inch from top of paper
- Article on a Web site
- Indent turnover lines 1/2 inch
- Online subscription service
- Library and date of access
- *UP* means "University Press"
- Unsigned encyclopedia article
- Full publication information and page number not needed, only edition and date
- Online subscription service
- Date of access; Web site URL

US Lacrosse, "Participation Survey 2007." Web. 9 Mar. 2009.
    <www.uslacrosse.org/pdf/07participationsurvey.pdf>

Vennum, Thomas, Jr. *American Indian Lacrosse: Little Brother of
    War*. Washington, DC: Smithsonian Institution Press,
    1994. Print.

"Women's Lacrosse." *The Book of Rules*. New York: Checkmark
    Books, 1998. Print.

Article in a book;
no author given

APPENDIX A

What Every Research Paper Writer Needs

When you write a research paper, you need three things that you cannot buy in a store or borrow from a library: curiosity, self-discipline, and perseverance.

In fact, the research paper assignment is designed to help you acquire these qualities if you do not already have them. As you work through Steps 1 through 10, pacing yourself to finish on time, you will be practicing the arts of self-discipline and perseverance.

You will need some tangible things, too, and they are easier to acquire. Besides a computer, you will need access to an unabridged or college dictionary, an easy-to-use thesaurus, and a grammar-and-usage handbook. You will probably find them in your school or local library or in your English classroom. However, it is a good idea to have a good college dictionary, a thesaurus, and a language handbook at home, too. (You can buy them used from an online bookseller.) They will come in handy for the rest of your life.

A College Dictionary

Many people talk about looking something up in "the dictionary" as if there is only one. But there are hundreds of dictionaries of the English language in print. Some are extremely good; others are not. A good college dictionary will help you find or check all the following.

- spelling
- capitalization
- plural forms
- irregular verb forms
- comparative forms for modifiers
- word origins (etymologies)
- idioms (expressions whose meanings differ from each word's literal meaning)
- level of usage (for example, colloquial, slang, archaic, poetic)
- usage notes
- synonyms and antonyms

- biographical entries (spelling, pronunciation, identification, birth and death dates)
- geographical entries (spelling, origin of name, location, population, sometimes a little history)

Listed below are three of the best hardbound college dictionaries available. Resist the temptation to buy or use a paperback dictionary. Paperback dictionaries have fewer entries and scanty definitions, and they tend to fall apart after minimal use. If you are buying a dictionary, be sure to buy a hardbound *college* dictionary, not a *school* dictionary for young students.

- *Merriam-Webster's Collegiate Dictionary.* 11th ed. Springfield, MA: Merriam-Webster, 2005.

This dictionary has over 225,000 definitions and more than 40,000 usage examples. It includes an 18-page style handbook that is based on the authoritative *Webster's Third New International Dictionary*. A CD-ROM of the 11th edition is also included. This dictionary is updated annually to reflect new words and definitions.

- *The American Heritage Dictionary of the English Language*, 4th ed. Boston: Houghton Mifflin, 2000.

This large-format dictionary has more than 350,000 entries and more than 4,000 illustrations and drawings. Usage notes and regional American English notes provide up-to-date information on how words are used today in speech and writing. Houghton Mifflin also publishes *The American Heritage Dictionary, Third College Edition*, a standard-sized dictionary with more than 200,000 entries and many usage notes.

- *Webster's New World College Dictionary.* Ed. Michael Agnes. 4th ed. Hoboken, NJ: Wiley, 2004.

This is the dictionary used by the Associated Press as the standard for spelling and punctuation. Unlike other college dictionaries, this one was not based on an existing unabridged or earlier dictionary. It includes an easy-to-use pronunciation key.

A Thesaurus

The word *thesaurus* (thi ´sȯr ǝs), from the Greek *thesauros*, literally means "a treasure." The lifetime hobby of Peter Mark Roget (rō ´zhā), an English doctor (1779–1869), was grouping words into categories. For fifty years, he organized all the English words he knew and could discover into more than a thousand different categories of words related in meaning. He published the first thesaurus—his *Thesaurus of English Words and Phrases*—in 1852.

In book form, a thesaurus is a dictionary of synonyms and antonyms. A thesaurus is useful when you are trying to think of different ways to express an idea, when you want to avoid repeating the same word over and over again, and when you are searching for the word that best fits a particular context or shade of meaning.

There are almost as many thesauri available as there are dictionaries. Some require you to use an index that lists several different categories (depending on the sense of the word you are using) where you may find synonyms in the book. These index-based thesauri are more difficult to use than a dictionary-type thesaurus, which simply lists an entry word and offers a variety of synonyms and antonyms.

There is no need to spend a lot of money on a hardbound thesaurus. Here are three good paperback versions that will serve you well:

- *Random House Roget's Thesaurus*. 4th ed. New York: Ballantine Books, 2001.

In this easy-to-use paperback thesaurus, more than 11,000 main entries are alphabetized (just as they would be in a dictionary) with more than 200,000 suggested synonyms and antonyms. This thesaurus is also available as an e-book.

- *The New American Roget's College Thesaurus in Dictionary Form*. Ed. Philip D. Moorehead. 3rd rev. ed. New York: Signet, 2002.

This paperback combines the dictionary-style alphabetical listing and occasional larger-type entries for categories (as in the original *Roget's Thesaurus*).

- *Webster's New World Thesaurus*. By Charlton Laird. 3rd ed. New York: Pocket Books, 2003.

This is another easy-to-use, dictionary style thesaurus. It was written by an expert on contemporary American language.

e-writing You may have available one of the many word-processing programs equipped with a thesaurus. When you highlight a word in the text, the thesaurus suggests one or more replacements. (Suggested substitutes for *reliable*, for instance, might include *faithful*, *dependable*, *unfailing*, and *trusty*.) But a computer thesaurus is much less reliable than a thesaurus in book form. Sometimes, it fails completely, as if it does not understand what you are asking it to do.

A Language Handbook

When you write, revise, and proofread your research paper, you will find a well-organized language handbook extremely useful. Unless you are confident that you know all of the rules for grammar, usage, punctuation, and capitalization (and who does?), it is a good idea to have a reliable "expert" to check with. Any of the hardbound handbooks listed here should last you a lifetime.

- Fowler, H. Ramsey et al. *The Little, Brown Handbook*. 10th ed. Boston: Longman, 2008.

This thorough, easy-to-use handbook starts out with a section on the writing process and paragraphs. It devotes sections to grammatical sentences, clear sentences, effective sentences, punctuation, mechanics, effective words, the research paper, and special writing tasks (essay exams, business writing). There are features for ESL (English as a second language) students throughout the handbook. At the back, there is a twenty-page glossary of usage, an appendix on preparing a manuscript, and another on writing with a word processor.

- Kirszner, Laurie, and Stephen Mandell. *The Holt Handbook*. 6th ed. New York: Harcourt, 2002.

This handbook is organized into nine parts, beginning with one on the writing process and paragraph skills. Succeeding sections deal with thinking critically, composing sentences, common sentence problems, using words effectively, grammar (with twenty pages on language issues for international [ESL] students), punctuation and mechanics, writing with sources, and writing in various disciplines.

A Book on Style

You can find dozens of books that attempt to teach the niceties of writing clear, graceful English. However, there is just one you should definitely read and—if possible—own:

- Strunk, William, Jr., and E. B. White. *The Elements of Style*. 4th ed. New York: Longman, 2000.

This slim book (only 128 pages) first appeared in 1918. The *New York Times* calls it "as timeless as a book can be in our age of volubility." The authors give rules, examples, and sage advice on points they consider essential to good writing. The book's five sections deal with elementary rules of usage, elementary principles of composition, a few matters of form, words and expressions commonly misused, and an approach to style. The style section offers twenty-one sensible rules, such as "Avoid fancy words" and "Place yourself in the background." You can find the full text of William Strunk's original edition of *The Elements of Style* (1918) online at <http://www.bartleby.com/141/>.

Writing Across the Curriculum

You may find a research paper assigned in your social studies or science class and sometimes in other classes, too. The movement to add substantial writing assignments in classes other than English is a result of a widespread effort to improve students' writing and thinking skills. The "writing across the curriculum" movement began in the 1970s and quickly became established at all levels, from elementary school through college. Teachers in subjects other than English generally give no instruction in how to go about writing research papers. They assume that you already know all you need to know from your English classes.

Usually, an assignment by a social studies or science teacher is quite specific. Here are two examples:

Social studies. Discuss the application of one amendment in the Bill of Rights to contemporary life. Cite at least one recent case heard before the Supreme Court. Summarize the arguments of both sides in the court case, and then state your own opinion.

Biology. Discuss one example of symbiosis among plants or animals. Explain how the organisms interact as well as the benefits and disadvantages of the relationship to each organism.

Sometimes, a teacher will ask you to choose a topic of particular interest to you that is, of course, related to what you have been studying. In that case, you will have to come up with a suitable topic and limit it appropriately. On the following pages, you will find several lists of broad, general subjects that may help you think of a topic for a research paper. These lists may be useful when you are searching for a topic for a paper for a social studies, science, or art class. They may also help you choose a topic for a research paper in your English class.

Inquiry-Based Research

The best kind of research paper starts with a question or questions that truly interest you, questions to which you would very much like to know the answers. Such research is called **inquiry-based**. The research that you do will be satisfying because you are motivated by your curiosity, your desire to find information to answer your very own questions. Here, for example, are several questions that could be researched and developed into a paper:

Biology. In some species of birds, the males and females are exactly alike in size, coloring, and marking; in others, the males and females are quite different. Why? What theories have been proposed to explain this fact?

Government. What are the arguments for and against English-only laws? Which position do I agree with, and why?

Earth science. Why are fossils found in some areas of the United States but not in others?

Economics. After several years of state-run lotteries in (name a state), what conclusions, positive and/or negative, can be reached? In what specific ways do the lotteries benefit (and/or not benefit) the citizens of the state?

THE WRITING PROCESS. Your teacher will probably want to approve the limited topic that you choose for your paper. Once your topic is approved, you will follow the same steps (Steps 2–10) outlined in this book for any type of research paper. The writing process is the same, no matter what the subject. You will need to find sources, gather information, organize your findings, and write the first draft. You will also need to allow plenty of time to revise and improve the first draft. If you keep to a timetable and follow the steps in the text, you should be able to turn in a carefully written paper for any class. For a science or a social studies class, the final product of your research may be something other than—or in addition to—a written paper. See Step 10 for information and ideas about publishing your research as a multi-media presentation, an oral report, or a pamphlet or brochure.

THREE PATTERNS OF ORGANIZATION. Here are three of the most common patterns of organization for research papers in various content areas.

Comparison/contrast. When you compare two or more things, you discover and describe their likenesses. When you contrast them, you tell how they are different. You may compare and contrast writers, artists, battles and other historic events, solutions to problems, species of plants and animals—you name it. As long as the two subjects have at least one important feature in common, you can develop a comparison/contrast paper.

Problem/solution. You are most likely to write this type of paper in a social studies class. You identify and describe a specific problem, discuss one or more possible solutions to that problem (or solutions that have actually been tried), and come to some conclusion about the effectiveness of those solutions. In this kind of paper, you will use the critical-thinking skill of evaluation. You will be expressing your own judgments about what does and does not work and about which solution is the best and which solution is the worst.

Cause/effect. This pattern of organization is most likely to be useful in science and social studies. You might write, for example, on some aspect of the environment or on how national and international news (good, bad, and in between) appears to affect the American stock exchanges. You can either analyze an effect (a situation or an event) to find its various causes, or you can start with a cause and write about its effects. Causes and effects are not always clear-cut; they are often a matter of interpretation. This type of paper tends to contain a lot of the writer's own thinking and speculation.

Social Studies

Social studies covers a broad range of subjects (and classes) having to do with the study of people. All of the following subjects are branches of social studies: history, government, geography, economics, anthropology, archaeology, sociology, and psychology.

PARTS OF THE PAPER. If you are writing for a social studies class, your teacher may want you to use the APA style of documentation (see Appendix C). Your paper will have a title page, an abstract (a brief summary of the main ideas covered in the paper), and an introductory paragraph. The body of your paper will be grouped under headings (such as "Methods," "Results," "Data," "Procedure," "Discussion," and "Conclusions"); and instead of a Works Cited list (MLA style) at the end of your paper, you will have a Reference List.

If you are writing a history paper, your teacher may require that you use one or more **primary sources**. These are documents written during the period you are writing about. The text of the Gettysburg Address is a primary source; so are letters written to President Lincoln and newspaper accounts that appeared at the time of Lincoln's speech at Gettysburg. (A **secondary source** in this case would be a historian's account of the importance of the Gettysburg Address or a literary critic's evaluation of the speech and its structure.) If you are writing a sociology paper, your teacher may ask you to include original primary sources such as an interview or a survey you create and conduct. Unlike research papers written for English classes, social studies papers often include figures, graphs, and tables. Such visuals are referred to in the text and appear close to the discussion or at the end of the paper.

REFERENCE SOURCES. On pages 22–25 you read about general reference sources. The reference sources listed here are specific to social studies. You are likely to find them in a public library, a local college or university library, a bookstore, or even online. They may be used for browsing, if you are trying to think of a good topic, or for research in the social sciences.

> *Africana: Civil Rights: An A–Z Reference of the Movement That Changed America.* Eds. Kwame Anthony Appiah and Henry Louis Gates, Jr. Philadelphia: Running Press, 2005.
>
> *Africana: The Encyclopedia of the African and African American Experience.* Eds. Kwame Anthony Appiah and Henry Louis Gates, Jr. New York: Basic Civitas Books, 2005.
>
> *Almanac of American History.* James Miller and John Thompson. Washington, DC: National Geographic, 2006.

Encyclopedia Latina: History, Culture, and Society in the United States. 4 vols. Eds. Ilan Stavans and Harold Augenbraum. Danbury, CT: Grolier, 2005.

Handbook of North American Indians. 20 vols. Ed. William C. Sturtevant. Washington, DC: Government Printing Office, 1978–2006.

Timelines of World History. John B. Teeple. New York: Dorling Kindersley, 2006.

Women's Studies Encyclopedia. By Helen Tierney. Rev. and expanded ed., 3 vols. Westport, CT: Greenwood, 1999.

You may find it easier—and more fun, too—to browse through stacks of recent back issues of magazines, looking for articles that suggest a topic. Try *Ebony, Smithsonian, American Heritage, History Today, Psychology Today,* and *National Geographic.* Or try browsing through the social studies section in a library or bookstore.

TOPIC IDEAS. The following general topic ideas need to be limited to a specific aspect that you can research with the sources available to you. If you find a general topic that interests you, use the limiting techniques (brainstorming, clustering, questioning, KWL) suggested in Step 1 to come up with a workable topic for your research paper.

- One event, invention, or movement that changed human history
- A Native American tribe—its culture, past or present
- Slavery in the Americas
- Racism
- Women's suffrage
- Women's issues today
- A period in history you would like to have lived in, and why
- What you would put in a time capsule
- What education was like in colonial America (or any other period and place)
- Patterns of immigration to the United States in a specific period
- The Great Depression
- The American labor movement
- Child labor in the United States; in other countries
- Minimum wage laws
- Juvenile crime/juvenile justice system
- Peer pressure
- Urban problems
- Homelessness
- People with disabilities
- Curfew laws
- English-only laws
- Census data
- Trial by jury
- Freedom of speech
- Guns in American society; in other societies
- Drug education
- Gangs
- Charities
- America's two-party political system
- Voter apathy

- Rights and responsibilities of citizens
- A Civil War (or Revolutionary War) battle
- Lewis and Clark expedition
- Early history of your town, city, or community
- A famous American speech
- An important/influential U.S. first lady
- Milestones in U.S. public education
- *Brown* v. *Board of Education* (or some other important Supreme Court decision)
- Cuban Missile Crisis, 1962
- An immigrant's experience on Ellis Island; on Angel Island
- Civil disobedience: Henry Thoreau; Mohandas K. Gandhi; Dr. Martin Luther King, Jr.
- The biggest problem in the world today

Science, Mathematics, Technology

In a science class, the term *research paper* may have an altogether different meaning than it does in a social studies class. Instead of a survey of information that others have written about a topic, a science research paper is sometimes a detailed report of the writer's original research. This research may take the form of a single experiment or a series of experiments conducted over a long period of time.

Each year, almost two thousand high school seniors submit research papers to the Intel Science Talent Search, a prestigious national competition. These students describe their original research (done under the sponsorship of a teacher and/or scientist) in one of the following categories: behavioral and social sciences, biochemistry, botany, chemistry, computer science, Earth and space sciences, engineering, environmental sciences, gerontology, mathematics, medicine and health, microbiology, physics, zoology, and team projects. Judges award more than $300,000 in college scholarships to finalists based on an evaluation of students' use of the scientific method, experimental procedures, and detail and accuracy of data presented. For an application, rules and regulations, and directions for writing a science research paper for this contest, see the Web site of Intel Science Talent Search (www.societyforscience.org/sts). On this same Web site, you can also get information about summer programs and internships throughout the United States for middle school and high school students interested in science, mathematics, and engineering.

Find out from your teacher if there are local or state competitions that you can enter. Extremely useful resources for students entering science competitions can be found in this book:

Cothron, Julia H., Ronald N. Giese, and Richard J. Rezba. *Students and Research: Practical Strategies for Science Classrooms and Competitions*. 3rd ed. Dubuque, IA: Kendall/Hunt Publishing, 2006.

PARTS OF A PAPER REPORTING ORIGINAL RESEARCH. In many respects, the parts of a science paper resemble the parts of a social studies paper. It has a title page and an abstract that summarizes in a page or less the research project or problem, poses the hypothesis (theory), the methods of research, and the results. The introduction includes a brief "review of the literature" (background information necessary to understand your project, including a summary of the most important and/or recent work on the specific topic).

The introduction is followed by a section on the experimental design (sometimes called "Methods and Materials") of your project. This needs to be detailed enough so that someone can repeat your study to see if the results are the same. Then comes a section on procedure (what you did, how you did it, how you measured it), followed by a section on your results, including tables of data, charts, and graphs, as well as paragraphs in the text describing your results. Finally, there is a section on your conclusions: the purpose of your experiment, your major findings, whether or not the findings support your hypothesis, and possible explanations for your findings. At the end, there is a list of works consulted in writing your paper.

REFERENCE SOURCES. Here are some reference sources you may use both for browsing, if you are trying to think of a good topic, and for research.

American Men and Women of Science. 26th ed. Farmington Hills, MI: Gale, 2009.

CRC Concise Encyclopedia of Mathematics. Eric W. Weisstein. 2nd ed. Boca Raton: CRC Press, 2002.

Gale Encyclopedia of Science. Ed. K. Lee Lerner. 4th ed. 6 vols. Farmington Hills, MI: Gale, 2007.

McGraw Hill Encyclopedia of Science & Technology. 9th ed. 20 vols. New York: McGraw, 2002.

Smithsonian Institution Earth. Ed. James F. Luhr. New York: Dorling Kinderseley, 2007.

Ultimate Visual Dictionary. New York: Dorling Kinderseley, 2006.

Van Nostrand's Concise Encyclopedia of Science. Eds. Alan Axelrod and Christopher G. De Pree. New York: Wiley, 2003.

If you enjoy leafing through magazines, try recent and back issues of these publications: *American Scientist, Audubon, Natural History, Nature, Science News, Scientific American,* and *Sierra: The Magazine of the Sierra Club.*

TOPIC IDEAS. Here are some general topic ideas:

- The single most important invention of the 20th or 21st century; what life would be like without it
- Predicting natural disasters
- Do animals feel and/or think?
- Animal communication
- Animal-rights activists
- Volcanoes
- Preventable deaths
- Endangered environments/species
- Black holes

- Patents/copyrights for scientific discoveries
- Which is more important: nature (genes) or nurture (environment)?
- Benefits of exercise
- Protecting children from accidents and hazards
- Tobacco, alcohol, and other drugs
- Ethical issues in research with human subjects
- Cell biology—latest research
- Math puzzles
- Probability
- Math as a tool
- Catalysts
- Global warming
- Life elsewhere in the universe?
- What's new in the solar system?
- An organism's responses to external stimuli
- Population growth
- DNA
- Gene therapy
- Newly discovered viruses
- Underwater research
- Hybrid cars
- Acupuncture
- Herbal medicine
- Industrial robots
- Computer software
- Internet issues
- Training of U.S. astronauts
- Fossil fuels—Are the world's resources running out?
- Andromeda galaxy
- Comets and asteroids
- $E = mc^2$
- Galileo Galilei
- Gravity
- History of the periodic table of the elements
- Light: What it is, how it works
- Mars (or any other planet)
- Solar and lunar eclipses
- Space telescopes
- Quantum mechanics
- Einstein's theory of relativity
- Sunspots
- Aurora borealis (Northern lights)
- Life on a coral reef
- Earthquakes
- Hurricanes
- What fossils tell us
- Ice Ages
- Radioactive dating
- Tornadoes
- Dinosaurs
- Metamorphosis: life cycles with radical change
- James D. Watson and Francis H. C. Crick
- Asthma
- Blood types
- Colorblindness
- Vitamins: What they do; why you need them
- Braille
- Rachel Carson and DDT
- Life on a space station

Literature, Music, Art

When you write a research paper for a humanities (as literature, music, and all the arts are called collectively) class, you will use the MLA format and the MLA style of documentation. You will follow Steps 1 through 10 of the text.

REFERENCE SOURCES. Here are some reference sources you may use both for browsing, if you are trying to think of a good topic, and for research.

The American Humanities Index (online database). EBSCOhost, 1918–present.

Benét's Reader's Encyclopedia. Ed. Bruce Murphy. 5th ed. New York: HarperCollins, 2008.

Contemporary Authors. Farmington Hills, MI: Gale, 1962–present.

Contemporary Literary Criticism. Farmington Hills, MI: Gale, 1973–present.

The Dance Handbook. Ed. Allen Robertson and Donald Hutera. Farmington Hills, MI: G. K. Hall, 1990.

Dictionary of Literary Biography (series). Farmington Hills, MI: Gale, 1978–present.

Gardner's Art Through the Ages. Ed. Fred S. Kleiner et al. 13th ed. Belmont, CA: Wadsworth, 2008.

The New Grove Dictionary of Music and Musicians. Ed. Stanley Sadie and John Tyrrell. 2nd ed. New York: Oxford UP, 2004.

The Oxford Companion to Music. Ed. Alison Latham. Rev. ed. New York: Oxford UP, 2002.

The Oxford History of Western Music. 6 vols. Richard Taruskin. New York: Oxford UP, 2005.

Magazines and journals that may be available in your library include *American Art Journal*, *American Music*, *Art & Antiques*, *Art in America*, *Architectural Digest*, *Dance Magazine*, *The New Yorker*.

TOPIC IDEAS. Here are some general topic ideas:

- Importance of one artist
- Compare/contrast two artists
- Harlem Renaissance
- Imagists (the movement in American poetry)
- American Romanticism (Realism/Naturalism/Regionalism)—movements in American literature
- Rock 'n' roll
- Reggae (or any other type of music)
- WPA (Works Progress Administration) during the Great Depression
- Analysis and evaluation of a literary work
- Analysis and evaluation of a specific painting, sculpture

- Eastern music
- Folk art/music/dance
- French Impressionists
- Batik (or any other art process)
- Depression glass
- *Animal Farm* by George Orwell
- History of the skyscraper
- Marian Anderson's life and work
- Milestones in photography
- Diego Rivera's murals
- George Eliot's life and work
- The fables of Aesop
- Totem poles
- The life and work of Jacob and Wilhelm Grimm, the "Brothers Grimm"
- Animé
- Invention of the alphabet
- The legend of King Arthur
- Emily Dickinson's life and poetry
- Origins of theater—ancient Greek theater
- John Henry (or any other American folk hero)
- Chaucer's *Canterbury Tales*
- Hans Christian Andersen's life and work
- *Don Quixote* by Miguel de Cervantes
- Franz Kafka's life and work
- *Gulliver's Travels* by Jonathan Swift
- The work of Frank Lloyd Wright (or any other architect)
- Homer's *The Iliad* (or *The Odyssey*)
- Louis Armstrong's life and work
- Jonathan Swift and "A Modest Proposal"
- Mark Twain's life and work
- Lewis Carroll and *Alice's Adventures in Wonderland*
- Sophocles' Oedipus trilogy
- The works of Dr. Seuss (Theodor Seuss Geisel)

APA Style; Footnotes and Endnotes

Throughout this book, we have used the MLA (Modern Language Association) style of documenting sources because it is the style that most English teachers prefer. It is, however, not the *only* style. If you are writing a research paper for a social studies or science class, your teacher may ask you to use the APA (American Psychological Association) style. Or you may be asked to document your sources with footnotes or endnotes. On the following pages, you will find rules and examples for each of these methods of documentation, as used in a student paper on the Cuban Missile Crisis.

Hint!

Be sure to find out which style your teacher requires *before* you begin taking notes (Step 3). All your source citations should follow the style rules and format *exactly*. Even a misplaced or missing comma or period may affect your grade.

APA Style

The APA style is described in great detail in the *Publication Manual of the American Psychological Association*. It is the style required for writers of college-level psychology and other social science papers and journal articles. It is also a style frequently used to report original research.

An APA-style paper has several elements that an MLA paper does not have.

1. It always has a **title page**. Centered on the title page are the paper's title, the writer's name, the course name, the instructor's name, and the date the paper is being submitted. A key phrase from the title appears as the running head on the upper right-hand corner of every page. The same phrase is centered toward the bottom of the title page. Pages are numbered, starting with 1 for the title page.

2. It always has an **abstract**, a concise summary of the main ideas covered in the paper. The abstract appears on its own page, after the title page and before the text of the paper. Often, the abstract is one long paragraph; its first sentence is *not* indented. The word *Abstract* is centered at the top margin (one inch from the top of the page). See the sample Abstract on the next page.

3. The text of the paper begins on the page following the Abstract page. The **text** is double-spaced, and each paragraph is indented. The paper's full title is centered at the top of the page. An introductory paragraph, which is not labeled with a heading, briefly introduces the topic of the paper and any findings or conclusions. Other sections of the paper may have headings, such as "Methods" (or "Methodology"), "Results," "Data," "Procedure," "Discussion," "Conclusions."

Abstract

    The Cuban Missile Crisis of October 16—28, 1962, threatened nuclear war but ended as an opportunity for peace. On October 16, President Kennedy received word that Soviets were building offensive missile bases in Cuba. Kennedy and his advisors spent six days deliberating what action to take. The public was not informed of the crisis until the evening of October 22, when Kennedy addressed the nation and announced a U.S. quarantine (blockade) of Cuba. After several tense days, during which nuclear war seemed a real possibility, Soviet premier Nikita Khrushchev withdrew the missiles from Cuba. The crisis was seen as a tremendous victory for the United States in the Cold War. It also spotlighted the fear of the real possibility of nuclear war. Two positive and lasting results of the Cuban Missile Crisis are the Limited Nuclear Test Ban Treaty of 1963 and the hotline established between the White House and the Kremlin.

4. Following the text is a **References** page or **Reference List**. It is an alphabetical list of all works cited in the text of the paper. Here are the APA rules for listing sources on the References page:

- Center the heading ("References" or "Reference List") two inches from the top of the page. Skip four spaces before the first entry.

- Double-space all entries. Use a **hanging indent**; that is, start the first line at the left margin, and indent all turnover lines for the same entry three spaces. (See the examples on page 186.)

- Alphabetize all entries by author's last name. If the author is unknown, alphabetize by the first important word in the title (not the articles *the, a,* and *an*). Write the author's last name, followed by a comma and the initial or initials of his or her first and middle names. End the author information with a period.

- For two authors, list each, giving the last name first. Use the ampersand sign (&) between the authors' names. For more than two authors, use a comma and the ampersand before the last author's name.

- Following the author's name, write the date of publication in parentheses. Place a period *outside* the closing parenthesis.

- Do not use quotation marks for the titles of chapters, articles, poems, or essays. Use regular type; do not underscore or italicize.

- Italicize titles of books, magazines, journals, and newspapers.

- For titles of all works cited, capitalize *only* the first word of the title and the subtitle (the word following the colon) as well as all proper nouns and proper adjectives. Keep all other words in the title lowercase, and end with a period.

- When citing publishers, use an abbreviated form for the publisher's name (for example, Doubleday, *not* Doubleday & Co.), but give the full name of university presses (for example, Columbia University Press, *not* Columbia UP).

If you record all the information you need in *exactly the right style* when you are writing your bibliography source cards, it will be easy to do your References page at the end of your paper. In APA style, authors' first names are not listed, only their initials. The citations also differ from MLA style in punctuation, capitalization, and placement of information. In the chart on page 186, you will find a summary of the difference between the APA and MLA styles.

It is important to note that, as is the case with any editorial style, APA style changes from time to time. To make sure you are using the most up-to-date APA style, it is a good idea to check the APA *Publication Manual* Web site at <http://www.apastyle.org>.

PART OF PAPER	APA STYLE	MLA STYLE
TITLE PAGE	Always has	Optional
ABSTRACT	Always has	Never has
RUNNING HEAD AND PAGE NUMBER	Key phrase from title; page number on line below running head (flush right at top of page): Cuban Missile Crisis 1	Writer's last name followed by page number on the same line (flush right at top of page): Porter 1
SOURCES LISTED AT END OF PAPER	References page. Indent turnover lines three space.	Works Cited list. Indent turnover lines five spaces.
Book by single author	Finkelstein, N. H. (1994). *Thirteen days/ninety miles: the Cuban missile crisis*. New York: Julian Messner.	Finkelstein, Norman H. *Thirteen Days/Ninety Miles: The Cuban Missile Crisis*. New York: Julian Messner, 1994. Print.
Book by two authors	Craig, G. A., & George, A. L. (1990). *Force and statecraft*. New York: Oxford University Press.	Craig, Gordon A., and Alexander L. George. *Force and Statecraft*. New York: Oxford UP, 1990. Print.
Book with single editor	Divine, R. A. (Ed.), (1971). *The Cuban missile crisis*. Chicago: Quadrangle Books.	Divine, Robert A., ed. *The Cuban Missile Crisis*. Chicago: Quadrangle Books, 1971. Print.
Unsigned magazine article	Showdown-Backdown. (1962, November 5). *Newsweek*, 28.	"Showdown-Backdown." *Newsweek* 5 Nov. 1962: 28. Print.
Magazine or newspaper article with one author	Reston, James. (1961, October 24). Khruschev's misjudgment on Cuba. *The New York Times*, p. 38.	Reston, James. "Khruschev's Misjudgment on Cuba." *New York Times* 24 Oct. 1962, sec. 1: 26. Print.

PARENTHETICAL CITATIONS

The APA author-date system of parenthetical documentation gives the author's last name, followed by a comma and the date of publication. When a specific page is referred to, a page number is also given. See the following example.

> A letter writer to the *Miami Herald* (Schwartz, 1962) soberly warned: "John F. Kennedy will go down in history as one of this country's great Presidents—or its last—as a result of the [October 22] speech."

Here are the rules for parenthetical citation in the APA style:

- Enclose in parentheses the author's last name, a comma, and publication date.

- When there are two authors, cite both authors' last names and connect them with an ampersand. For more than two authors, give each one's last name, followed by a comma. Use an ampersand before the last author's name.

- Cite the page number(s) when a specific part of the work is referred to. Use *p.* (for "page") or *pp.* (for "pages") before the page numbers.

- When an author's name appears within the sentence of the text, do not repeat it in the parenthetical citation.

- When the author is unknown, the parenthetical citation should give the first important word or words in the title of the work enclosed in quotation marks.

PARENTHETICAL CITATIONS	APA STYLE	MLA STYLE
Book by single author	(Finkelstein, 1994)	(Finkelstein 109)
Book by two authors, specific page	(Craig & George, 1990, p. 129)	(Craig and George 129)
Book by three or more authors	(Bullock, Stallybrass, & Trombley, 1995)	(Bullock, Stallybrass, and Trombley)
Book by single editor, specific page	(Divine, 1971, p. 154)	(Divine 154)
Magazine or newspaper article (signed)	(Robertson, 1962)	(Robertson)
Magazine or newspaper article (unsigned)	("Blockade," 1962)	("Blockade")
Encyclopedia article (unsigned)	("Munich," 2001, p. 1857)	("Munich")

Footnotes and Endnotes

Before the 1980s (when parenthetical citations were first introduced), all research paper writers used either footnotes or endnotes to document their sources. With these systems, quotations or paraphrases that need documentation are indicated by a superscript (raised) number following the quotation or paraphrase. This number refers the reader to the place where full information about the source is given. When the full documentation appears at the bottom of the page, it is called a **footnote**. When it appears on a separate sheet at the end of the paper, it is called an **endnote**.

Today, footnotes and endnotes are only used for additional comments or explanations that would interrupt the flow of the text. Used for this purpose, they are called **content notes**.

    News of the crisis first reached the American public
on the evening of October 22, when Kennedy addressed the
nation on radio and television.[9] (It is eerie to look back
at newspapers and magazines from October 16—21, when life
seemed totally normal while the urgent probability of
nuclear war was being discussed in the White House.) The
President detailed the discovery of Cuban missile bases,
announced the U.S. quarantine of Cuba, and promised that
the U.S. would take further action if necessary....

[9.] Security at the White House, the State Department, and the
Armed Forces was extremely tight and effective; there were
no leaks to the press or news media.

If you were to use **endnotes** instead of footnotes, all of your numbered comments would appear on a separate sheet (or sheets) of paper entitled "Notes" immediately before your Works Cited page.

GUIDELINES FOR PLACEMENT OF FOOTNOTES AND ENDNOTES

Both footnotes and endnotes

- Number the footnotes or endnotes consecutively throughout the paper.

- Place a superscript (raised) Arabic number immediately *after* the punctuation mark following a quotation or paraphrase.

Footnotes only

- Separate the footnote(s) from the text of the paper with four lines of space or with a twelve-space rule from the left margin (as in the example on page 188).

- Indent each footnote five spaces. Start turnover lines at the left margin. Begin with the superscript number, *followed by one space*.

- Single-space the text of each footnote. If more than one footnote appears on a page, use two lines of space (a double space) between footnotes.

Endnotes only

- List all endnotes, numbered consecutively, on a separate page or pages at the end of the paper.

- Center the word *Notes* one inch from the top of the page. Use three lines of space between this heading and the first note. Unlike footnotes, endnote entries are double-spaced.

- Indent each note five spaces. Turnover lines are flush left with the margin. Begin with the superscript number, *followed by one space*.

INDEX

Exercises are indicated by numbers in *italics*.

R

S

T

U

V

W